Great Bike Rides

in
Eastern
Washington
& Oregon

Sally O'Neal Coates

WILDERNESS PRESS
BERKELEY

Dedication

To my husband, Doug,

and the thousands of miles of road ahead.

FIRST EDITION May 1996

Copyright © 1996 by Sally O'Neal Coates
Book design by Margaret Copeland
Cover design by Larry Van Dyke
Photos and maps by the author except as noted
Cover photo: *The Palouse, Washington* © 1996 by John Clement

Library of Congress Card Catalog Number 96-7797
International Standard Book Number 0-89997-200-4

Manufactured in the United States of America

Published by   Wilderness Press
               2440 Bancroft Way
               Berkeley, CA 94704
               (800) 443-7227
               Fax (510) 548-1355

               Write, call or fax for free catalog

Library of Congress Cataloging-in-Publication Data

Coates, Sally O'Neal
    Great bike rides in eastern Washington and Oregon / Sally O'Neal Coates. -- 1st ed.
        p.   cm.
    Includes index.
    ISBN 0-89997-200-4
    1. Cycling--Washington (State)--Guidebooks. 2. Cycling--Oregon--Guidebooks.
    3. Washington (State)--Guidebooks. 4. Oregon--Guidebooks. I. Title.
    GV1045.5.W2C63 1996   96-7797
    796.6'09795--dc20   CIP

Table of Contents

Rides In Order of Difficulty

Acknowledgements

Scores of people helped make this book a reality. Chief among them were my writing group, Marilyn Morford and Diane Molleson, without whom the book would not have been started, and my husband, Doug, without whom it would not have been finished. I thank my family and friends for putting up with my absence. Special thanks for the support of my "inner circle"— you know who you are.

Finally, thanks to staff members of Chambers of Commerce, City Halls, Forest Service and National Park offices throughout Washington and Oregon, and thanks to members of the communities through which I rode, who gave of their time to answer my questions. Some have been acknowledged by name within the individual rides. To those whose names I missed, my thanks are every bit as sincere: the gentleman in the café in Silver Lake, the woman in the book store in Joseph, the two little boys in Heppner, the ranger at Fort Spokane, and all the rest. Thanks again.

Introduction

This is a guidebook for moderately proficient recreational bicyclists looking for good cycling routes in eastern Washington and Oregon states. Why eastern Washington and Oregon? Those who have ridden here know—the "forgotten" area east of the Cascade Mountains is ideal for bicycling. The basins and foothills of eastern Washington and Oregon offer wide-open spaces, outstanding scenery, friendly small towns, and miles on end of flat or gently rolling terrain. Add to that a flourishing wine industry, a few tourist-savvy towns like Spokane and Pendleton, and plenty of old west and Native American history, and you have the makings of a great vacation.

The rides in this book have been selected with variety and fun in mind. They offer good cycling for a range of skill levels, and should prove interesting for the tourist, whether native or visiting the Northwest. Most of the routes begin, pass through, or are near a site of historical, recreational or geological significance designed to make your trip even more enjoyable before, during and after the ride.

Each ride has been assigned a level of difficulty, as follows:

- ● Easy: less than 20 miles.
- ■ Intermediate: 20 to 45 miles.
- ▲ Challenging: over 45 miles or with difficult hills.

On this basis, the book contains twelve ● Easy rides, fourteen ■ Intermediate rides and seven ▲ Challenging rides. (Several of the twenty-five numbered rides offer more than one route. The Wenatchee-Chelan ride, Ride 3, can be considered one challenging ride or two intermediate rides.)

This is a bicycling guidebook first and foremost, but additional information has been provided in some cases on lodgings, restaurants and other amenities, as well as on tourist attractions. The information is in no way intended to be inclusive, and is always subject to change. Telephone numbers are provided to help you acquire up-to-date information.

Road conditions are noted on most rides, and were accurate at the time of publication. Names of roads, bodies of water, and other landmarks were determined through a combination of map review and on-site research. Where information differed from one source to another, the guidebook relies on on-site observation or the information common to the greatest number of sources. Every effort has been made to make each route description and map detailed and accurate. In some instances, maps were derived from composites and are not precisely to scale; this is indicated on the map.

The rolling wheatfields of the Palouse

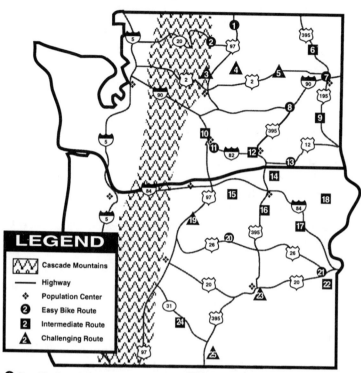

LEGEND

〰	Cascade Mountains
—	Highway
❖	Population Center
❷	Easy Bike Route
❷	Intermediate Route
▲	Challenging Route

❶ **Oroville Can-Am Tour** & Orchard Loop

❷ **Winthrop-Twin Lakes Loop**

▲❸ **Wenatchee-Chelan Overnight**

▲❹ **Grand Coulee Double Dam**

▲❺ **Davenport-Fort Spokane Loop**

❻ **Waitts Lake-Chewelah Scenic**

❼ **Best of Spokane**

❽ **Ritzville Ride**

❾ **Palouse Tour from Colfax**

❿ **Selah-Naches Valley**

⓫ **Yakima Valley Wineries**

⓬ **Richland/Benton City Loop**

⓭ **Walla Walla Stateline Loop**

⓮ **Helix Wheat Country**

⓯ **Heppner Rollers**

⓰ **Ukiah to Hot Springs**

⓱ **Baker City Loop &** ● **Mini-Loop**

⓲ **Wallowa Lake Scenic**

⓳ **Ghost Town Gulch**

⓴ **Fossil Follies**

㉑ **Vale-on-the-Trail**

㉒ **Owyhee Loop**

▲㉓ **Harney Valley Big Ol' Flat (&** ■ **)**

㉔ **Silver Lake Forest Loop**

▲㉕ **Lakeview Out-and-Back**

Reminders
for a Safe and Fun Ride

A few simple preparations can mean the difference between an enjoyable ride and disaster. Take time to review and follow these guidelines, and remember to obey the rules of the road.

Preparation and Gear
- Make sure your bike is in proper working order: brakes, chain, cables, etc. Check it before each ride, and have a professional tune-up once a year.
- *ALWAYS* carry water. The eastern Washington and Oregon climate is bone-dry, and the evaporation rate can make the reality of perspiration deceptive. Drink before you're thirsty, and top off your bottles at every safe opportunity. Distances between watering holes can be far, so mount extra bottles or carry a pouch.
- Carry patches or spare tubes, tire irons, air pump and hex wrenches; also 25¢ for an emergency phone call (or, better yet, a cell phone if you have one!).

Clothing
- Wear brightly colored clothing, and consider strips of reflective tape for your clothing, bike and helmet.
- *ALWAYS* wear a helmet.
- Wear eye protection against sun and insects.
- Don't let floppy pant legs or shoelaces become caught in your chain—tie them up.

Rules of the Road
- Bicycling is allowed on most roads in eastern Washington and Oregon, even some of the interstate and posted limited-access highways. The main exceptions are around population centers such as Spokane. If in doubt, check the local telephone directory for the area in which you will be riding, and call the local office of the State Patrol.
- Ride single file when automobiles are present.
- A bike is considered a vehicle under Washington and Oregon state laws, and is subject to the same rules as an automobile (stop signs, traffic lights, turn procedures, etc.) Especially important to remember:
- Ride WITH traffic, never against it.

- Use hand signals for turns and lane changes: Left arm straight out for left turn, right arm straight out for right turn, left arm out and bent downward at the elbow for stop.
- Do not pass on the right.
- Do not turn left except from the left lane (alternately, dismount and walk your bike, using pedestrian crosswalks).

Common Sense

- Avoid riding at night; if you must, have proper illumination and lots of reflective tape.
- Avoid riding over gratings, drains, and subsurface maintenance holes.
- Cross railroad crossings and cattle catchers at a right angle or walk your bike. (For the uninitiated, "cattle catchers" are a series of metal bars crossing the road with a ditch under them, designed to discourage livestock from crossing by catching their feet/hooves.) In this guide, railroad crossings and cattle catchers are indicated in the Ride Descriptions.
- Be alert for gravel and debris in the roadway, especially on shoulders and turns. As most of eastern Washington and Oregon is subject to snow in the winter, early spring riders should be especially aware of the traction sand and gravel that was deposited during the winter.

Remember to obey the rules of the road

ᘔᘔ 1 ᘔᘔ
Oroville Can-Am Tour & Orchard Loop

● Easy, Can-Am Tour — 18.2 miles
● Easy, Orchard Loop — 7.2 miles

Can-Am tour is fairly flat, with optional very steep
10-mile out-and-back spur. Orchard Loop is gently rolling.

Highlights

Can-Am Tour: sparkling Lake Osoyoos, the U.S./Canadian border crossing, the communities of Oroville, Washington, and Osoyoos, British Columbia. Orchard Loop: Oroville town and countryside, the Similkameen and Okanogan rivers.

General Descriptions

Both rides begin and end in the community of Oroville, located on Highway 97 a few miles south of the Canadian border. The Can-Am Tour loop is a relaxing and unique ride on good surfaces that takes you north on 97 across the border into British Columbia. Loop through the town of Osoyoos, then hook back up with Highway 97 to return to Oroville the same way you came. Good roads, farm and orchard scenery, and views of Lake Osoyoos throughout the ride. With the exception of a grueling and optional 10-mile hill climb at the turnaround point (which takes the ride from "easy" right into "challenging"), the course is fairly flat.

The short Orchard Loop is an attractive jaunt along the hillside over Oroville past scattered homes, orchards, and lake access roads. Moderately good surfaces and some slight hills. Suitable for all ages and abilities.

Start

As Highway 97 goes through town, it becomes Main Street. Both rides begin at the Washington State Visitor Information Center on the west side of Main, behind which is the Oroville City Park with restroom facilities and parking.

Can-Am Tour

[0:4] MILEAGE LOG

0.0	**Turn left** out of the parking lot of the Visitor Center. You are turning across highway traffic (although the speed limit is only 25mph here), so use caution.
0.25	Begin ascending a 3/4-mile incline.
0.4	Osoyoos Lake State Veteran's Memorial Park Recreation Area on your right. Portions of the Osoyoos River/Osoyoos Lake delta area have been visible on your right; as you continue to ascend, the lake itself becomes visible. As you reach the top of the rise, you can see Copper Mountain on your immediate left and Kruger Mountain ahead and slightly to the left. Continue north on Hwy. 97, a well-paved two-lane highway with a shoulder. A narrow strip of vineyards and orchards separates you from the lake on the right.
4.0	Enter the commercial clutter just south of the border crossing.
4.6	US/Canadian border crossing. Bicycles may cross in the same manner as automobiles. Bring a photo ID and be prepared to stop and answer questions. Do not bring fresh fruit or vegetables across the border (eat those bananas in advance!)
4.8	Sign reads OSOYOOS – 5 KM, PENTICTON – 68 KM. Keep an eye peeled for the ostrich farm on the left. Orchards on both sides of the road.
6.0	Commercial development; dining and lodging opportunities. Fork in the road. **Take the right fork** toward Osoyoos Town Centre. Follow 89 St. as it slopes downhill for about 1/2 mile into town.
6.6	Another fork. **Take the right fork**, following the edge of the lake, and winding through a residential area. A wide margin on the side of the road allows for easy cycling, but is also used for automobile parking, so exercise caution.
7.0	Stop-sign intersection with 83t. Turn right.
7.1	Cross Lake Osoyoos, which is divided between a southern and a northern portion at this point. Then enter into a resort section of town, rife with family-style restaurants and economy lodgings bearing names like Sun Beach and Surf Side. The north shore of the south portion of the lake forms a beach on your right all along this section.
7.6	The first in a series of produce markets on your right, followed by a grocery store.

| 8.0 | Touch of Holland Gift Shop, Coffee Shop and Bakery on your left. You can't miss the giant windmill. Across the street is a nice, open, grassy picnic spot. |
| 8.4 | **Y** in the road; main road curves to the left, narrower 62nd Ave. to the right. Fruit stands on both sides of the road. **This is the turnaround point** for the main ride. |

OPTIONAL 10-MILE SCENIC SPUR

Hardier souls (and I do mean hardy—this is Ironman stuff) might wish to take the left fork and continue up the steep and winding hill that eventually affords a spectacular view of Lake Osoyoos, the town of Osoyoos, and all the way back across the border. A right-hand pull-out occurs 4.6 miles up, followed by the first good opportunity to turn around, a left-hand pull-out at 5 miles. Not for your average recreational cyclist—the climb is grueling and the descent hair-raising.

8.4	Turn and retrace your route through the fruit stands and resort area.
9.5	The lake shore is on your left, separated from the road by a strip of grassy park. This is a good spot to stop and wait for any "Ironmen" in your party who decided to climb the hill. If your plans call for lunch north of the border, you can choose from the resort area offerings here or wait until you go through downtown Osoyoos in less than a mile.
9.7	Cross the separation between north and south Lake Osoyoos again.
9.8	Kingfisher/Lakeshore intersects on the left. **Continue straight** on 83 St. towards downtown Osoyoos.
10.1	**Turn left**, following the sign for British Columbia Hwy. 3 West to Penticton. Be careful as you proceed through this busy section of downtown Osoyoos. It is a small town, but this is a central shopping strip with pedestrian and vehicle cross traffic.
10.4	Osoyoos town hall on the left.
10.5	Road curves to the right and inclines slightly uphill as you leave town. **Work your way into the left lane**, following signs for the junction with Hwy. 97 South. (NOTE: Depending upon traffic, you might wish to remain in the right lane and walk your bike across the intersection coming up at the stop light.)
10.9	**Turn left** at the stop-light intersection with Hwy. 97.
11.7	Elks Lodge on your right.

11.8	**Y** in the road. **Take left fork**, continuing on the main road, 97 South.
12.2	Road leading back into Osoyoos intersects on your left. **Continue straight.**
12.8	Road intersects on the left, leading to Haynes Point Provincial Park. **Continue straight.**
13.6	Road forks for border crossing. **Take the right fork.** Duty-free shop with Canadian souvenirs, restrooms.
13.8	Border crossing.
14.3	Sign indicates that Oroville is 4 miles ahead. Hwy. 97 from here back to Oroville is a relaxing, gradual descent.
17.7	Entering Oroville sign.
18.2	Back to Washington State Visitor Information Center.

Orchard Loop

MILEAGE LOG

0.0	**Turn right** out of the parking lot of the Visitor Center. Cruise down Main St., through a portion of the northern downtown section of Oroville.
0.45	**Turn right** on 12th Ave., following sign towards Wannacut Lake.
0.6	Road curves to the left, passing a school and ballfield on your left (home of the "Oroville Hornets"—does that tell us anything about airborne wildlife in the Oroville area during harvest time?).
0.7	Cross the Similkameen River, just north of where it joins the Okanogan River.
0.85	Gayes Pt. Rd. intersects on the right. **Continue forward** on a shoulderless, two-lane highway. Residential density thins and agricultural activity increases as you proceed on this uphill grade away from town.
1.4	**Turn right**, following signs toward cemetery, Golden Rd., Ellemeham Mountain and Wannacut Lake.
1.6	**Y** in the road. **Take the left fork** onto Golden Rd. toward Wannacut Lake. Right fork was Ellemeham Rd. A rock-faced hill rises on your right as you proceed down Golden; farm and orchard land are below on your left. The roadway, while still paved, is slightly rougher here, with no shoulder and no markings.
2.0	Oroville Riverview Cemetery entrance on your left. **Continue straight** up a short steep rise.

2.5	90° bend to the right, followed by 90° bend to the left. Be aware that these are working orchards; be attentive to cross traffic.
3.3	Intersection on the right. Sign indicates that Wannacut Lake, Blue Lake and Sun Cove Resort are up this road. **Continue straight.**
3.5	90° bend left begins a series of **S**-curves as the route heads back toward the river.
3.75	Stop sign at **T**-intersection. Tonasket is to the right, Oroville to the left. **Turn left.**
4.2	After a series of **S**-curve, the Oroville Gun Club is on your right. The Similkameen and Okanogan rivers are now in view on your right as you begin retracing your route back to town.
5.7	Road to the cemetery on your left.
6.3	Gayes Pt. Rd. intersection on the left.
6.4	Recross the Similkameen River and enter Oroville city limits.
6.65	Stop-sign intersection. Penticton (BC) to your left and Wenatchee (WA) to your right. **Turn left.**
6.8	WELCOME TO OROVILLE sign on your right.
7.2	**Turn left** into Visitor Center.

Other Activities In and Around the Route

Both Oroville and Osoyoos are lovely small communities with stunning four-season scenery and adequate tourist amenities for an extended stay. The Osoyoos Chamber of Commerce (604-495-7142) lists 17 motels, 9 bed & breakfasts, and 10 campgrounds with RV hook-ups. Oroville offers lodgings as well, and camping at Osoyoos Lake State Veteran's Memorial Park (86 sites, phone 509-476-3321). Oroville's Chamber can be reached at 509-476-2739.

Entertainment in this area is largely outdoor-oriented and low-key. It is a good area for walking and cycling. Things "heat up" in the summer, when Osoyoos offers resort activities including a water slide, miniature golf, scooter rentals, parasailing, and horseback riding. Paddle boats, jet skis, and other watercraft are available for rent at the various marinas along the lake. The amphitheater at Haynes Point Provincial Park offers informative naturalist talks suitable for all ages, and you need not be a guest of the park to participate.

In the winter, tourist activity quiets down, but the area is still beautiful. Sitzmark ski area is only 17 miles east of Oroville, and Mt. Baldy is 40 miles from Osoyoos.

Oroville's once-busy Great Northern railroad depot, at the south edge of town, west of Main, is now a museum attesting to this area's rich history. History buffs will also enjoy the town of Molson, whose museum is located in an early 1900's school house and also displays an outdoor collection of early pioneer buildings and equipment. Reach Molson by heading about 9 miles east on the Oroville-Toroda Creek Road, then about 5 miles north on Molson Road.

Spring and fall are fishing time. Osoyoos Lake is home to 15 species of fish, most notably rainbow trout and bass, and can be fished from the shore or by trolling or casting from a boat. This heavily orchard-covered area is especially beautiful in April and early May, when the fruit trees are in blossom. From June through October, you can enjoy the seasonal fruits of these same orchards at the many fruit stands.

If you wish to spend more time north of the border, consider a trip up to Penticton, BC, only about 45 miles north of Oroville. Site of many British Columbia events and conventions, including the Canadian Ironman triathlon each August, Penticton is tourist-friendly and offers a wide variety of activities and information for your stay.

Oroville welcomes visitors

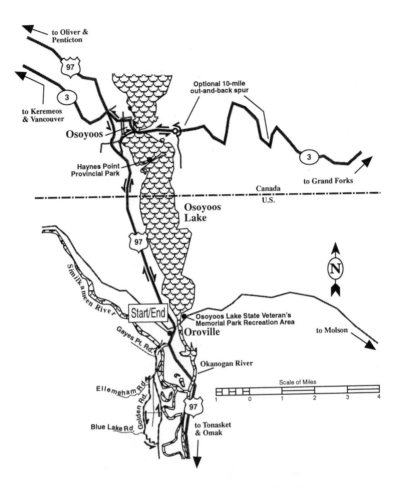

Oroville Can-Am Tour & Orchard Loop

● Easy, Can-Am Tour — 18.2 miles (——)
● Easy, Orchard Loop — 7.2 miles (- - - -)

☙ **2** ☙
Winthrop-Twin Lakes Loop

● Easy — 18.2 miles

Mostly flat. Skipping the Pearrygin Lake out-and-back spur
results in a very short, easy 9.5-mile loop.

Highlights

The historic town of Winthrop, Pearrygin and Twin lakes, and
the Chewuch and Methow rivers, all nestled in the pine-ringed
Methow Valley.

General Description

Easy, scenic loop through the timbered Methow Valley,
between two sections of the Okanogan National Forest amongst
the foothills of the Cascade Mountains. Winthrop is at the east
end of the North Cascades Highway, considered one of
Washington's most scenic roads.

Start

The loop begins in historic downtown Winthrop. Winthrop is
situated on Highway 20, the North Cascades Highway. It is 98
miles north of Wenatchee and 61 miles north of Chelan.
Entering from the eastern side of the state, Highway 20 West
goes northwest into downtown, makes a left, crosses the
Chewuch River, then bends right. Shortly following the bend,
on the left, is the gravel parking lot of the Methow Valley Visitor
Center. The ride begins from this parking lot.

🚲 MILEAGE LOG

0.0	**Turn right** as you leave the parking lot of the Methow Valley Visitor Center.
0.05	Pass The Barn community center on your right.
0.1	Road bends to the left, crossing the Chewuch River just north of where the Chewuch joins the Methow River.
0.2	**Turn right** at the stop sign, following Hwy. 20 southeast through historic downtown Winthrop. The Methow River runs along your right as you leave town.

0.7	**Road curves right**; cross the Methow River. Patterson Mountain looms straight ahead.
0.8	Fork in the road. **Take the right fork**, Twin Lakes Rd., rather than the left fork, which would be the continuation of Hwy. 20. A school is on your right after the fork.
1.1	Horizon Flat Rd. intersects on the left; **bear right**, continuing on Twin Lakes Rd.
1.2	Winthrop National Fish Hatchery access road on the right. The road enters a series of **S**-curves.
2.2	Wolf Creek Rd. intersects on the right. Continue on Twin Lakes Rd., up a winding incline.
3.0	Twin Lakes Drive intersects on the left; sign for Sun Mountain Ranch. **Continue straight.**
3.9	The Twin Lakes, two small fishing lakes surrounded by pines, become visible on your left.
4.1	**Y**-intersection. Patterson Lake Rd. goes off to the right (6.4 miles to Sun Mountain Lodge, see *Other Activities In and Around the Route Area*). **Take the left fork**, continuing on Twin Lakes Rd. as it curves to the left and around the south side of the Twin Lakes.
4.6	Methow Valley Rodeo Arena on the right.
5.2	Wandling Rd. intersects on the right. The road continues east and slopes downhill toward Hwy. 20.
6.0	**T**-intersection. Liberty Bell High School on the right. Twisp is to the right, Winthrop to the left. **Turn left** onto Hwy. 20, exercising caution, as this is the area's main highway. Roadway is rough due to summer-winter temperature shifts and precipitation.
6.45	**Fork right** onto Witte Rd., a narrow, somewhat rough but beautiful road along the Methow River paralleling Hwy. 20.
7.4	Stop-sign intersection with Hwy. 20. **Turn right** back onto the highway toward town.
7.8	ENTERING WINTHROP sign. This is the newer part of Winthrop; commercial services and lodgings can be found here as well as along the historic downtown corridor.
8.45	Farm House Inn Bed & Breakfast on your left.
8.7	Road curves to the right to re-cross the Methow River and retrace part of your original route.
8.8	**Turn left** after the bridge, continuing on Hwy. 20 back into town.

9.1	Entering historic downtown Winthrop.
9.2	Duck Brand Hotel & Cantina on your right.
9.3	4-way stop. To proceed to Pearrygin Lake, **continue straight** ahead. For a shorter ride, turn left and re-cross the Chewuch River to the starting point.
9.5	With the John Wayne Building directly in front of you, the road bends 90° to the right and begins an ascent. From here to Pearrygin Lake, the road is narrow, somewhat rough, and inclines gradually but steadily all the way. The Chewuch River valley is visible below on your left.
11.0	**Turn right**, following sign for Pearrygin Lake Recreational Areas.
11.5	Silverline Resort road intersects on your right, immediately after which Pearrygin Lake becomes visible on your right.
12.0	Derry's Resort road descends toward the lake on your right.
12.8	**Turn right** on Pearrygin Lake Rd. *CAUTION:* "Cattle catcher" grating immediately following the turn. *WALK YOUR BIKE.*
13.6	Park registration booth and **turnaround point.** For mileage purposes, turn your computer off here and restart upon leaving the booth for the return trip. The approximately 3/4-mile road back out of the park is uphill.
14.4	**Turn left** at the stop sign. It's all downhill from here.
16.2	T-intersection with E. Chewuch Rd. **Turn left**, following sign back toward Hwy. 20 and Winthrop.
17.2	CITY LIMITS sign.
17.7	Back at the John Wayne Building, on your right as you come to the bottom of an incline. Road makes a **90° left turn** to take you back into town.
17.9	Back at 4-way stop in downtown Winthrop; **turn right.**
18.0	Cross Chewuch River, then curve to the right. After the curve, stay left when the road forks.
18.1	**Turn left** into the Visitor Center.

Other Activities In and Around the Route Area

The Methow Valley is an awesome year-round recreation area: from mountain biking and horseback riding in the summer to world-class cross-country skiing and snowmobiling in the winter. And when you're tired of outdoor recreation, the tiny town of Winthrop (pop. 324) is full of antique and gift shops to keep you busy in its "old west" style restored downtown.

The cycling season in Winthrop begins in April with the annual opening of the North Cascades Highway (providing access from the west), and culminates in a Mountain Bike Festival in October. But why should off-road cyclists have all the fun? While paved roads are few in the sparsely populated Methow Valley, traffic is light, and services are plentiful. And the people of the area have a great attitude toward tourists.

Lodgings are plentiful in Winthrop. The Duck Brand Hotel offers clean, spare, pine-furnished rooms overlooking the south end of the quaint downtown. Farm House Inn, operated by the Duck Brand, is located on the other side of the river and farther south. The Inn has a selection of rooms with private or shared bath, a common living area, and a hot tub. Reach either at 1-800-996-2192. Sun Mountain Lodge (1-800-572-0493), while not necessarily the most logical jumping-off point for a touring road cyclist (being several miles from town up rough Patterson Lake Road), is an experience not to be missed. Both the resort and the restaurant have earned AAA's 4-diamond rating—try to at least have dinner there. For more lodging choices, contact the Winthrop Chamber of Commerce at 509-996-2125.

The Duck Brand Cantina, downstairs from the hotel, is another super dining experience. From their aromatic, fresh-ground Starbucks coffee and fresh baked pastries in the morning to their hearty and unique dinner choices (Mexican, pasta, ribs, chicken), you could eat there for a week and not get bored. Fat, perhaps, but not bored.

Pearrygin Lake State Park (509-996-2370) is 578 acres of rolling foothills centered around natural, spring-fed Pearrygin Lake. With 83 campsites (30 with full hook-up), the park offers fishing, swimming, boating, and waterskiing in the summer. Most park facilities are closed November 15 through March 31.

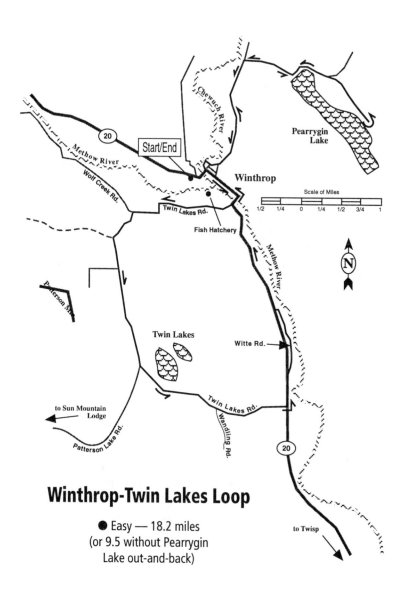

Winthrop-Twin Lakes Loop

● Easy — 18.2 miles
(or 9.5 without Pearrygin
Lake out-and-back)

᪣ **3** ᪣
Wenatchee-Chelan Overnight

▲ Challenging — 87.9 miles
(in two parts, 43.0 miles and 44.9 miles)
Rolling road with two major climbs.

Highlights

The cities of Wenatchee and Chelan, the Columbia River, and Lake Chelan.

General Description

This ride shows off the best of eastern Washington: from the world-famous orchards of Wenatchee (apple capital of the nation), up the mighty Columbia River to beautiful Lake Chelan, and back through the serene Douglas fir, ponderosa pine and cedar of Wenatchee National Forest. The route is somewhat hilly with two steep climbs, one on either side of Chelan. The community of Chelan provides a picturesque opportunity for an overnight stay, with all the amenities of a major resort area.

Thanks to members of the Apple Capital Bicycle Club of Wenatchee 509-886-0585 and to the Wenatchee Sunrise Rotary for sponsoring an annual century ride and assisting in defining this excellent route.

Start

Begin at Confluence State Park, the northernmost of a series of Wenatchee parks along the west bank of the Columbia River. Abundant parking makes this a good jumping-off point for a long ride; if you plan an overnight stay in Chelan, a parking fee will apply ($5.00 in 1996). The ride starts at the park check-in/fee collection booth.

0⁄4 MILEAGE LOG

0.0   Leave the check-in/fee booth, head **uphill and out of the park** to the north.

0.2   Stop sign at the top of the park exit drive. **Turn right** on Old Station Rd., then **almost immediately turn left** on Isenhart. The mile from the park to the highway winds through a fruit-packing industrial area; be alert for turns.

0.5	**Turn left** at **T**-intersection stop sign (Euclid Ave.).
0.55	RR Crossing and stop sign.
0.6	Stop sign. **Turn right** on Penny Rd.
0.9	Washington Apple Commission Visitor Center on your left. Follow the signs for East Hwy. 2 toward Okanogan/Spokane (get in the **left lane**). **Enter the highway**, staying on the shoulder and exercising caution, and proceed up the incline to cross the river.
1.4	Begin crossing the Columbia River. Road continues to incline. Prepare to turn left at the **T**-intersection after the bridge at the top of the incline. **Turn left**, following Hwy. 2/97 East towards Spokane/Okanogan. This good, two-lane road with narrow shoulder takes you through orchard land and high sagebrush desert with almost constant views of the Columbia River all the way to Chelan.
7.2	Convenience store/gas station on right.
7.4	Rocky Reach Dam access and Lincoln Rock State Park on your left, along with another convenience store. Restroom facilities. Rocky Reach Dam includes an art gallery, geology displays, an electrical museum and fish viewing. Lincoln Rock (so named for the rock out-cropping across the river, said to resemble our 16th president) offers camping, boating, swimming and restrooms.
10.4	Lake Entiat overlook pull-off on the left.
14.3	ENTERING ORONDO sign.
15.0	**Y** in the road; café. Hwy. 2 East goes off to the right toward Waterville. **Continue north (straight)** on Hwy. 97.
16.6	Orondo Elementary School on the left.
17.7	Orondo Park on the left, on the river. Restroom facilities.
21.4	Begin a 3/4-mile steeper incline. Daroga State Park is visible on your left.
21.8	Entrance to Daroga State Park.
26.7	Brays Rd. intersects on the right. **Continue straight.**
37.0	Sign for BEEBE BRIDGE & STATE PARK.
37.7	Access road to Beebe Bridge Park on your left. **Continue straight** to cross bridge.
38.0	Cross the Columbia River on the Beebe Bridge.
38.3	**Turn left**, toward Chelan via Hwy. 150 West.

38.5	RR Crossing, followed immediately by a sharp bend to the left.
38.8	Chelan Falls Park on your left. Begin a long, steep, winding ascent into Chelan. Excellent (and well-earned!) views of the river valley as you ascend.
40.3	Top of the worst part of the ascent, as you enter an industrial fruit packing area. Still climbing.
41.5	**T**-intersection; stop sign. Top of the hill! Alternate Highway 97 North toward Okanogan to the right; **turn left** on Alt. Hwy. 97 South toward Chelan, Wenatchee and Manson. You can now see the sparkling waters of Lake Chelan, straight ahead.
41.7	Chelan Middle and Senior High on your right; entering Chelan. The road you are on is now called Woodin Ave.
42.3	Sanders St. intersection; signs indicate turns toward South and North Shore Recreation Areas. **Go straight** ahead and follow the road as it bends left to cross the picturesque bridge that separates the Chelan River (on your left as you cross) from Lake Chelan (on your right).
42.8	Wenatchee National Forest Ranger Station on the right. (You are still on Woodin Ave.)
43.0	**T**-intersection where Woodin meets Webster Ave. Turn off computer. End of first ride.

Second Half, or Day Two

[0⊞] MILEAGE LOG

0.0	Begin at the **T**-intersection of Woodin and Webster avenues. Head west on Alt. Hwy. 97 South (turning right off Woodin at the **T**) toward the south shore of the lake, which you will skirt for the first portion of the ride.
0.5	Slidewaters waterslide park and Waterslide Drive intersection.
0.6	Chelan Airways airplane tours on the right, followed immediately by the Lady of the Lake passenger ferry to Stehekin at the north end of the 55-mile lake.
2.2	Lake Chelan tourist information sign on the right.
2.7	First sign mentioning Lake Chelan State Park. We will be following signs toward this park.
3.3	**Take right fork** toward Hwy. 971 South/Fields Point Landing, continuing along the south shore of Lake Chelan as Alt. Hwy. 97 peels off

and heads south. Residential development along this section necessitates caution due to driveways and crossroads.

9.55	Lake Chelan State Park on the right; camping, boating, swimming, waterskiing, scuba diving.
9.6	**Turn left** on Navarre Coulee Rd., the continuation of Hwy. 971. This begins the most infamous stretch of the Wenatchee Apple Capital Century, a winding, steep climb through the edge of the Wenatchee National Forest back to Alt. Hwy. 97 South. The two-lane road is well-paved, with shoulder in places. Stunning views of the lake as you catch your breath on the hairpin turns.
11.0	You made it! The worst climb of the day is behind you. Now enjoy a mile-long downhill. The scenery changes from forested ranchland to high desert dotted with orchards.
18.3	Another nice downhill as you descend toward Alt. Hwy. 97.
18.6	*CAUTION:* tight left-hand curve begins a series of **S**-curves in your final descent toward the highway and the Columbia River.
19.2	**T**-intersection with Alt. Hwy. 97. **Turn right** to head south along the Columbia River and the Burlington Northern railroad tracks. The ride back to Wenatchee from here is a net downhill.
23.0	Vast volcanic cliffs in front of you are Ribbon Cliffs, part of Ribbon Mesa.
24.3	Historical marker on the right, commemorating Earthquake Point, site of a violent earthquake in December 1872.
25.35	ENTIAT CITY LIMITS.
28.0	Entiat State Park on the left.
28.5	Access road to Entiat River Recreational Area on the right.
28.7	Cross the Entiat River.
37.8	Vista Point on the left, overlooking Lake Entiat, the name given to this part of the Columbia behind the Rocky Reach Dam.
39.6	Rocky Reach Dam Visitor Center and Fish Viewing turnoff on the left.
43.0	Access to Ohme Gardens County Park on the right. This 9-acre alpine-style garden park is situated on a rocky bluff with spectacular views of the river, the valley, and the Cascade Mountains.
43.4	Hwy. 2/Seattle exit forks to the right; **continue straight**, under the overpass. Using caution, move into the left lane.
43.9	Right lane exits toward Hwy. 2/Spokane. **Continue straight**, retracing your route to Confluence State Park.

44.3	**Turn left** onto Euclid Ave. , followed by railroad crossing.
44.4	**Turn right** onto Isenhart.
44.6	T-intersection; **turn right** onto Old Station Rd., then immediately **turn left** into Confluence State Park.
44.9	Ride ends back at park fee station.

Other Activities In and Around the Route Area

Wenatchee and Chelan both offer plenty of options for an extended visit. While in Wenatchee, jog, stroll, or take a short, family-friendly bike ride on the Apple Capital Recreation Loop Trail, a paved 11-mile loop that follows the Columbia River on both the Wenatchee and East Wenatchee sides. From April 15 through October 15, visit Ohme Gardens, just north of town. In the winter, Mission Ridge ski area is only 12 miles away. Contact the very active Wenatchee Chamber of Commerce at 509-662-2116 for additional tourist information.

Several bike shops in Wenatchee serve an increasing number of resident and touring cyclists. Those with high recommendations from locals include Asplund's, Full Circle, and Second Wind. Second Wind, located on 9th Street NE just off Valley Mall Parkway (at the east end of the Columbia River footbridge), is also a cross-country ski shop and is adjacent to a fine espresso booth.

Near Wenatchee (west on Highway 2 toward Seattle) is the charming "Bavarian" village of Leavenworth, where restaurants, shops, and a year-round calendar of festivals offer some of the most authentic *gemütlichkeit* this side of Munich.

Chelan offers the advantages of a fully equipped resort community alongside the pristine wilderness of the lake itself. Obtain more information from the Chamber of Commerce at 509-682-3503. The active tourist will find all manner of diversions in town: from parasailing, jet-skiing, and river rafting to waterslides, bumper boats, and go-karts, to fine dining, shopping, and casino gambling. Those seeking an escape from it all will appreciate the unspoiled upper reaches of the lake. Lake Chelan is 55 miles long and 1486 feet deep (the third deepest lake in America), and roads extend less than halfway to its head. The town of Stehekin, as well as much of the lake shore, is accessible only by boat, float plane, and mountain trails.

Campers will appreciate the abundance of state parks between Wenatchee and Chelan. Lincoln Rock has Columbia River access and 27 campsites (509-884-8702). Lake Chelan State Park is right on the lake and offers 151 campsites (509-687-3710). The ride's starting point, Confluence State Park at the north end of Wenatchee, will begin offering camping on a reservation system in 1996. Phone 1-800-452-5687.

Lake Chelan

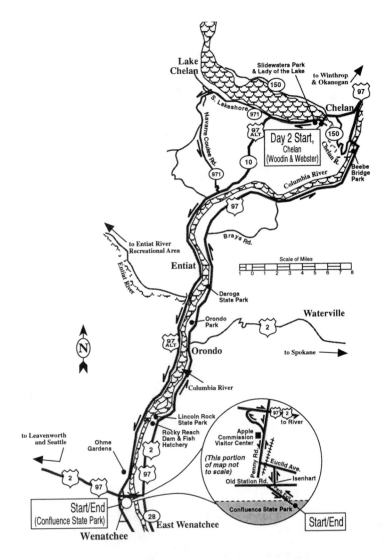

Wenatchee-Chelan Overnight

▲ Challenging — 87.9 miles
(in two parts, 43.0 miles and 44.9 miles)

⚙ **4** ⚙
Grand Coulee Double Dam

▲ Challenging — 83.9 miles
Rolling hills.

Highlights

Grand Coulee Dam and Dry Falls Dam crossings, towns of Coulee Dam, Grand Coulee, and Coulee City; views of Banks Lake and Steamboat Rock.

Route Description

This challenging course offers a variety of terrain and interesting sights, all on well-paved and lightly traveled highways. Take plenty of water, because towns are few and far between. Begin by crossing the mighty Grand Coulee Dam, heralded in song as the "biggest thing built by the hand of a man." Proceed to the town of Grand Coulee, where you begin a 5-mile climb onto a grassland plateau. The next 40 miles, along highways 174 and 17, are dry and deserted but pleasantly rolling, without steep hills. Intersecting with Highway 2, you cross Dry Falls Dam, pass Coulee City (an opportunity for a lunch stop), and head north along the east shore of Banks Lake. The final 30 miles are scenic and slightly hilly, passing recreation areas including Steamboat Rock State Park. Return to the start via the towns of Electric City and Grand Coulee, re-crossing the top of Grand Coulee Dam and descending into the town of Coulee Dam.

Since this ride crosses over the top of Grand Coulee Dam twice, it would be a good idea to check and see if the top of the dam road is open before heading out. Phone the dam Public Relations office at 509-633-9503 or the VAC/Visitor Arrival Center at 509-633-9265. The road occasionally is closed for maintenance work. If the road is closed, alternatives include starting and ending the ride in the town of Grand Coulee (in which case you miss the dam itself, but can drive down to see it after your ride); starting and ending at the VAC on the west side of the dam (where parking is limited and the ride begins and ends with a steep, congested segment of Highway 155); or starting as below, but heading farther west on Mead until it curves left into Roosevelt, crossing the Columbia River on the little bridge north of the dam, then turning left and following 155 up and out of the town of Coulee Dam (past the VAC).

This ride could also be approached as an overnight ride. Coulee City can be the starting point or the overnight point, with the other end in Coulee Dam, Grand Coulee or Electric City.

Start

Begin in the town of Coulee Dam, which straddles the Columbia River north of the dam. Start from the east side of town, where ample public parking is available along 6th Street, just north of and parallel to Mead Way and Roosevelt Way, the main east-west roads. Mileage calculations begin on Mead Way directly in front of the Colville Confederated Tribes Indian Museum and Gift Shop, a prominent A-frame structure. Just across the street is the north end of a park from which the dam can be viewed; the park has restroom facilities.

ⓞⓜ MILEAGE LOG

0.0	From the Indian Museum, **turn west** (toward the park, information station, and bridge) down Mead Way.
0.1	**Turn left** on Fir Street, then **another immediate left**, through a gate (this gate is closed when the top of the dam road is closed). The road doubles back past the A-frame museum where you began the ride.
0.25	Stop-sign **T**-intersection. VISITOR ROUTE to the left, PUBLIC FISHING to the right. **Turn left** up a gentle incline and into a **U**-shaped curve that takes you up to the east end of the top of the dam.
0.95	**Turn right** past a parking lot and onto the top of the dam. As you cross, it is an almost eerie feeling being atop this mega-source of hydroelectric power. See *Other Activities* for more information about the dam and tours. Be aware that the road atop the dam is pocked with gratings and concrete seams. None are big enough to catch a tire, but the result is a bumpy ride.
1.3	After angling southwest across the first section of the dam (the area below you is the Third Powerplant), you curve to the right and begin to head due west across the main section of the dam. As you cross, the city of Coulee Dam is below and on your right and Lake Roosevelt is on your left.

2.0	Stop-sign **T**-intersection with Hwy. 155. VAC/Visitor Arrival Center is downhill and to your right. To your left are Grand Coulee and Coulee City. **Turn left** and up a 0.3 mile hill.
2.3	Access to scenic viewpoint on your left.
2.9	Information signs and pull-off point on your left.
3.15	Entering the town of Grand Coulee.
3.65	**Turn right**, following signs for Hwy. 174 West/Bridgeport. Begin about a five-mile climb. Road is two-lane, moderately well-paved, mostly shoulderless.
4.6	Grand Coulee RV Park on your left; to your right, you can catch final glimpses of the Columbia River and the dam.
5.6	Crown Point Vista is off to the right.
8.1	Switchyard Rd. intersects on the left. Shortly afterward, the climb levels off. As you look across the parched plains, you begin to understand the importance and the magnitude of the Columbia Basin Project, the irrigation system that utilizes Grand Coulee Dam to turn a million arid acres into a breadbasket.
10.0	Smith Lake Rd. intersects on the right.
13.7	Barker Canyon Rd. intersects.
15.0	Begin a half-mile incline, followed by a series of rollers.
15.8	McCabe Rd. intersects on the right.
20.85	Del-Rio Rd. intersects.
23.05	S NE intersects on the right.
23.1	Half-mile uphill, followed by 2 miles of downhill to the Hwy. 17 junction.
25.7	**Turn left** onto Hwy. 17 toward Coulee City.
28.4	Begin a half-mile uphill. Gentle inclines and declines follow.
33.4	Hwy. 172 West to Mansfield intersects on the right. The east-west roads intersecting along this route are numbered in descending order as you head south; this road is also known as 14 NE. A few of these intersections are noted on the map for reference.
43.8	Begin descending into Haynes Canyon.
44.7	Pass under major power lines as you continue descending toward Dry Falls Dam and Coulee City.
47.75	Stop-sign **T**-intersection with Hwy. 2. To the right is West 2/Wenatchee; to the left is East 2/Spokane and the continuation of 17 south to Soap Lake. **Turn left.** Pavement is good, with wide shoul-

ders. As soon as you turn left, you can see the deep-cut gorge of the Dry Falls/Lower Grand Coulee. The road slopes downhill.

49.4 | Hwy. 17 south turns off to the right toward Soap Lake, Ephrata, and the Dry Falls Interpretive Center. Although our route **continues straight ahead** on Highway 2 toward Coulee City, be sure to take time to visit the Dry Falls Interpretive Center, just 2 miles south of this junction.

49.5 | Begin crossing Dry Falls Dam. To your right is the massive gorge of Dry Falls; to your left is Banks Lake, a recreational area and vital reservoir.

51.2 | ENTERING COULEE CITY. Coulee City Community Park to your left. Great spot for a shady picnic overlooking Banks Lake.

51.5 | Access road into Coulee City to your right. If you wish to visit this friendly town for lunch, picnic groceries, or just to walk Main Street and stretch your legs, turn off your computer at this junction and turn right. Otherwise, **continue straight** ahead on Hwy. 2. The next eight miles are basically flat.

53.4 | An unmarked road intersects from behind and to the right, as the route curves around 90° to the left.

53.8 | Highway 2 forks off to the right; **continue straight** on Highway 155 north toward Coulee Dam. This begins the most scenic part of the ride; you will be flanking Banks Lake for most of the remainder of the route. Not only is the lake beautiful, but the glacially-scoured gorge of the Upper Grand Coulee results in majestic basalt cliffs and outcroppings all along the lake.

59.7 | First of many public fishing access points on your left. Begin the first hill since Coulee City, about a mile in length.

61.5 | Begin a mile-long downhill.

63.0 | Around this point, the flat-topped bulk of Steamboat Rock is visible ahead, appearing to rise out of Banks Lake.

67.9 | Unmarked view point pull-off on the left; photo opportunity for Steamboat Rock.

69.8 | Left-hand access into Steamboat Rock State Park. As you proceed straight ahead on Hwy. 155, the bay between you and Steamboat Rock is knows as Devil's Punch Bowl.

71.4 | Gibraltar Rock ahead and on the right. Eagle Rock ahead and on the left.

72.2 | HISTORY OF THE STEAMBOAT ROCK AREA historical marker on the left.

73.25	Access to a rest area on your left. Dead ahead and straight up is Castle Rock.
73.45	Cross Northrup Creek.
74.2	Pass pyramid-shaped Eagle Rock on your left.
77.2	Airport Road intersects on the left.
77.5	Begin crossing Osborn Bay Lake.
78.1	Immediately after crossing the lake, access to Sunbanks Resort and RV Park on your left.
78.4	Entering Electric City. The road you are on becomes Coulee Blvd. Watch for cross-traffic in town.
79.2	Coulee Playland and Park on your left.
79.7	Entering Grand Coulee.
79.8	Rest Area access on the left. Proceed down a gentle downhill into town. Return to the intersection of highways 155 and 174, from which you accessed 174 west earlier in the ride. **Continue straight** on 155, retracing your route through town.
81.0	Entrance to information area overlooking Lake Roosevelt on your right. Grand Coulee Dam becomes visible on the right as the road curves left and downhill.
81.6	Scenic overlook pullout on the right.
81.9	**Turn right** to cross back over the dam. (If the dam road is closed— an infrequent occurrence during tourist season—you could continue straight on 155, dropping down the hill, passing the VAC and entering the west part of the town of Coulee Dam. Due to the steep pitch, curves and traffic of 155, the top of the dam route is more highly recommended.)
82.7	Still atop the dam, the road bends to the left to cross the Third Powerplant.
82.9	Road bends to the right, then comes to a stop-sign intersection. **Turn left** to wind back into Coulee Dam.
83.65	**Turn right**, following the VISITOR ROUTE sign, immediately after which the A-frame museum is visible on your right.
83.8	Gate and stop sign. Go through the gate, then **turn right**.
83.85	Immediately **turn right** again, onto Mead.
83.9	End of ride at the Indian Museum and Gift Shop.

Other Activities In and Around the Route Area

Grand Coulee Dam is an awesome achievement, a structure that cannot be described without the use of superlatives: the largest all-concrete structure in the world (many other dams are earth-filled); second greatest power-producing dam in the world (first is Guri Dam in Brazil, built more than 45 years later); site of the world's largest laser light show. The VAC/Visitor Arrival Center on Highway 155 just north of the dam is open year-round, with extended hours in the summer. A laser light show on the massive spillway of the dam is offered free of charge nightly from Memorial Day through September 30. And be sure to tour the dam itself, including the incline elevator in the Third Powerhouse, which travels 465 feet down the face of the dam on a 45° incline. The schedule of guided and self-guided tours varies, so call the VAC at 509-633-9265 for current information.

Fishing fans will enjoy the variety of lakes near the dam. Lake Roosevelt, the dammed up section of the Columbia River south of Grand Coulee Dam, is fished for kokanee salmon, walleye, smallmouth bass, net-pen-reared trout, and even sturgeon. Banks Lakes, the reservoir north of Dry Falls Dam, is outstanding for walleye, large- and smallmouth bass, yellow perch, and lake whitefish. South of Dry Falls, fish for trout at Blue Lake, Dry Falls Lake, and Perch Lake. A bit farther south on Highway 17, just north of Soap Lake, 1670-acre Lake Lenore is known for trophy-sized cutthroat. Be sure to purchase a fishing license and to check current restrictions before fishing.

If you enjoy the water but prefer not to fish, take a dip in the waters of Soap Lake, 21 miles south of Dry Falls Dam on Highway 17. The mysterious properties of this mineral-rich water have drawn claims of relief from ailments ranging from arthritis to psoriasis to circulatory and nervous disorders. Full tourist amenities are available in the town of Soap Lake. Contact the Chamber of Commerce at 509-246-1821. Lodgings and restaurants are also available in Coulee City (509-632-5713), Coulee Dam, Grand Coulee, and Electric City (509-633-1370).

Camping spots include state parks Steamboat Rock (8 miles south of Grand Coulee) and Sun Lakes (7 miles southwest of Coulee City), with 100 and 209 campsites, respectively, and a host of private campgrounds and resorts.

Finally, be sure to stop at the Dry Falls Interpretive Center, 2 miles south of the Highway 2/17 junction. Dry Falls shows stunning evidence of one of history's greatest waterfalls—three and a half miles wide and over 400 feet high (Niagara Falls is a mile wide with a 165-foot drop). The Interpretive Center explains how an Ice Age glacial dam re-routed the ancient Columbia River to carve what is now known as the "channeled scablands," a series of gashes in the vast lava plateau that is today's central Washington. Dry Falls and the Grand Coulee are among the most impressive features of the scablands.

U.S. Bureau of Reclamation

Grand Coulee Dam: the largest concrete structure in the world

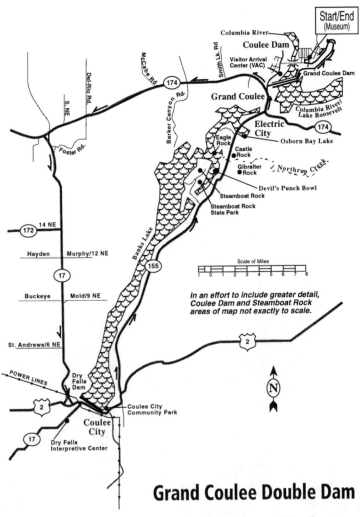

Start/End
(Museum)

Columbia River
Coulee Dam
Visitor Arrival
Center (VAC)
Grand Coulee Dam
Columbia River/
Lake Roosevelt

Grand Coulee

Electric
City   174
Osborn Bay Lake

Eagle
Rock
Castle
Rock
Gibralter   Northrup Creek
Rock
Devil's Punch Bowl
Steamboat Rock
Steamboat Rock
State Park

McCabe Rd.
Smith Lk. Rd
174
Barker Canyon Rd.
Del-Rio Rd.
S. NE
Foster Rd.

Banks Lake

172   14 NE
Hayden   Murphy/12 NE
17
Buckeye   Mold/9 NE

St. Andrews/6 NE

POWER LINES
Dry
Falls
Dam
2
Coulee
City
17
Dry Falls
Interpretive Center

Coulee City
Community Park

155

Scale of Miles
1   0   1   2   3   4   5   6   7   8

In an effort to include greater detail,
Coulee Dam and Steamboat Rock
areas of map not exactly to scale.

2

N

Grand Coulee Double Dam

▲ Challenging — 83.9 miles

ᗝᕀᗢ 5 ᗢᕀᗝ
Davenport-Fort Spokane Loop

▲ Challenging — 64.2 miles

Hills.

Highlights

Community of Davenport, Hawk Creek Falls, Fort Spokane, views of the Columbia and Spokane rivers (Lake Roosevelt), and pristine wilderness scenery.

Route Description

Beginning on Highway 2, this route heads west through gently rolling wheat fields and grasslands from the pleasant community of Davenport toward Creston. After almost 20 miles, you turn off onto another two-lane, reasonably well-paved road that winds up and down hills into scenic, forested canyons on the way to Fort Spokane at the confluence of the Columbia and Spokane rivers. En route, you pass Hawk Creek Falls and Campground (a short distance off the route) and Seven Bays resort and marina. After touring historic Fort Spokane, return to Davenport via well-paved and rolling Highway 25.

Start

Davenport is situated at the junction of Highway 2 and state highways 28 and 25, about a half hour west of Spokane. Straddling Highway 2, which is Morgan Street as it passes through town, Davenport extends for 3-4 blocks north and 8-9 blocks south. The town is 14 blocks wide and laid out along a regular grid with numerical streets running north-south (except "Harker," named for the area's original homesteader) and streets with names running east-west. The ride begins at the City Park, surprisingly enough located on Park Street (one block south of and parallel to Morgan), between 6th and Harker. Parking is available alongside the park.

0️⃣ MILEAGE LOG

0.0	Begin at the corner of 6th and Park. **Turn right** (north) on 6th.
0.1	Stop-sign intersection with Hwy. 2/Morgan St. Use caution as you **turn left**.
0.3	Historic Queen Anne-style house on the left, at 1001 Morgan.
0.45	Blinking-light intersection. Hwy. 28 to Harrington intersects on the left. Davenport Motel ahead on the left; Safeway grocery store on the right. **Continue straight** on Hwy. 2.
0.6	Ellie's restaurant on the left. Leave town on Hwy. 2 heading west toward Creston. Two-lane, well-paved road takes you out into gently undulating wheat fields.
4.6	Bottom of a descent, begin a 0.4 mile ascent.
6.0	Rocklyn Rd. intersects (both directions).
7.8	Road intersects on the left.
9.3	Road intersects on the right.
9.35	Road intersects on the left. Burlington Northern railroad tracks begin flanking the road to the left.
13.5	Rest Area on the left.
13.95	Telford Rd. intersects (both directions).
19.5	**Turn right** on Miles-Creston Rd.. As the route doubles back toward the east, stands of pine trees begin appearing. This road has steeper hills, beginning with about 2 miles of downhill, taking you into a meadowed valley ringed with pines.
22.7	Road for Lincoln, an abandoned sawmill site, intersects on the left. **Continue straight**, following the sign for Seven Bays.
24.35	Another road intersects on the left.
24.8	Road curves 90° to the left (first of a series of five 90° bends).
25.3	Wide curve 90° to the right.
26.5	Another 90° curve to the left.
27.5	In the midst of a grove of pines, another 90° bend to the right. A road intersects on the left at the apex of this bend.
28.3	Final 90° curve to the left.
28.7	Begin a long descent into Olsen Canyon. The pine and birch woods become thicker over the course of this nearly three-mile descent.
31.55	Cross Hawk Creek.

31.65	Hawk Creek Falls and Campground access road forks to the left just after the bridge. Begin winding uphill as you continue toward Fort Spokane. The climb out of the Hawk Creek area is neither as steep nor as long as the descent in.
33.5	Crest of the first hill; sweeping vista of the Roosevelt Lake section of the Columbia River ahead, just south of its confluence with the Spokane River. Watch for the totem pole on your left.
34.0	Access to Seven Bays marina and resort on the left. This privately operated facility offers camping, swimming, fishing, boating, and houseboat rental. Also features a grocery store and restaurant. Phone 509-725-1676. From here, as you wind basically downhill to Fort Spokane, individual homes and housing developments begin to dot the landscape.
36.2	Deer Meadows Golf & Country Club access on the left.
38.2	**Y**-intersection; **stay left** on main road. Begin final 3/4-mile descent to Hwy. 25 junction.
39.1	Stop-sign **T**-intersection. Fort Spokane and Kettle Falls to the left, Davenport to the right. Fort Spokane Store and Restaurant on your left at the junction. **Turn left** toward the fort.
39.5	Road intersects on the right, followed by COULEE DAM NATIONAL RECREATION AREA/FORT SPOKANE sign.
39.65	**Turn left** into Fort Spokane and head for the Visitor Center (see *Other Activities* for more information on the fort).
40.0	Stop your mileage computer at the Visitor Center parking lot and re-start after visiting the fort and enjoying the spectacular views of the mighty Spokane and Columbia rivers. Return to the highway using the same road on which you entered.
40.3	Stop-sign intersection with Hwy. 25; **turn right** toward Davenport. The first 6.5 miles out of Fort Spokane are uphill.
40.85	Back at the junction of Miles-Creston Rd. and **Highway** 25. Store and restaurant on the right. Proprietor is knowledgeable about the area. The store stocks bait, tackle and basic groceries (including bottled water for the climb back to Davenport), and the restaurant puts out a hearty meal for a fair price. Open 8am to 10pm. Leaving the junction, you head up a fairly steep, mile-long hill.
43.15	Road intersects on the right, immediately followed by one on the left. Similar intersecting roads, unnamed and often marked DEAD END intersect at intervals over the next few miles and are not mapped.

46.5	Begin a decline. Straight ahead is the picturesque Christ Lutheran Church, white with a green roof and steeple.
47.05	Church access road on the right.
47.6	Tall six-pack of grain elevators on your left; road curves to the right. You are now back in gently rolling farmland, having left the forested canyons behind.
51.3	Road to Porcupine Bay intersects in a **Y** from the right and behind. Road curves to the right and heads due south.
53.8	Gale Rd. intersects on the left.
56.9	Intersection: Larene Rd. to the right, Hansen Rd. to the left.
58.7	Chase Rd. intersects on the right.
58.8	Teel Hill Rd. intersects on the left.
63.55	Entering Davenport.
63.75	Stop-sign intersection with Hwy. 2. **Turn right.**
63.95	Edna's Drive-In on the right.
64.1	**Turn left** on Harker.
64.15	**Turn right** on Park.
64.2	Ride ends at City Park.

Other Activities In and Around the Route Area

Fort Spokane, the last of the frontier army posts, was established in 1880 to replace Fort Colville, a major fur-trading post to the north. From the outset, a primary function of the fort was to impress the white man's order upon the native Nez Perce, Sanpoil, and Nespelem people. At its peak in the 1890's, the Fort included over 50 buildings, three of which still stand today, including the massive quartermaster barn you see on your left as you enter the fort grounds. Renewed efforts toward maintenance and construction at the fort in recent years promise even more sights of historical interest. The strategic location of the fort at the confluence of the rivers results in an attractive park setting that includes picnic and swimming areas, a campground, fish station, dump station, and boat launch. Consult the Visitor Center for current programs put on by the National Park Service rangers who operate the park.

As you look out over the confluence of the Spokane and Columbia rivers, you are also looking at Lake Roosevelt, a 150-mile long recreational paradise created by Grand Coulee Dam.

According to a 1994 publication of the National Park Service, the lake is home to over 30 species of fish, including walleye, white sturgeon, yellow perch, kokanee salmon, and rainbow trout (trout populations maintained by net-pen rearing projects). Check with the Department of Fish and Wildlife in Spokane (509-456-4082) for current fishing restrictions in place. For a copy of "Lake Roosevelt: Official Map and Guide" and other information, call the Coulee Dam National Recreation Area at 509-633-9441.

Camping tends to be the lodging of choice for Lake Roosevelt visitors, with 35 campgrounds scattered about the lake. National Park Service campgrounds, of which there are 18, have picnic tables and restrooms, but no utility hookups. Closest motels to Fort Spokane are in Davenport and Kettle Falls.

Davenport is a charming community with several worthwhile sights of its own, as well as lodgings and restaurants. The Davenport Motel (509-725-7071) is smoke-free, spotless, economical, and conveniently located at the Highway 2/Highway 28 junction. Edna's Drive-In, at 3rd and Highway 2/Morgan, flips a great burger and makes memorable homestyle shakes, and Jungle Java does a fine job as the ubiquitous drive-through espresso stand that every Washington city with a population over 500 seems to offer.

Historic buildings in Davenport include the state's first school (a tiny log cabin on 7th), the stately Lincoln County Courthouse at 5th and Lincoln (partially destroyed by fire in late 1995), and homes at 9th and Marshall, 1001 Morgan, and 6th and Sinclair.

Also in Davenport is the Lincoln County Historical Museum a block south of Highway 2/Morgan at 7th and Park. Exhibits include an old-time country store re-creation, a farm equipment display, and period furniture and clothing. Hours are 9am to 5pm Monday through Saturday and 1 to 5pm on Sundays, May 1 through September 30. The Davenport Visitor Information Center (509-725-6711) is housed in the same building.

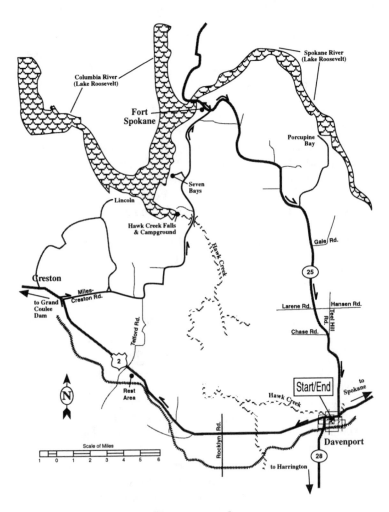

Davenport-Fort Spokane Loop

▲ Challenging — 64.2 miles

ᛠᛠ **6** ᛠᛠ
Waitts Lake-Chewelah Scenic

■ Intermediate — 29.6 miles

Scenic, with somewhat rough roadway.
Hilly and winding in places.

Highlights

Waitts Lake, the towns of Chewelah and Valley, and top-notch farm and forest scenery.

General Description

This ride is all about scenery: some of the most beautiful in the state. Situated in a bucolic valley between two tongues of the Colville National Forest, the Chewelah area is where the forest meets the fields. All points on the route have views of forest, farms, mountains, or all three. Midway through, the route loops Waitts Lake (see *Activities In and Around the Route Area*).

Surfaces are uniformly mediocre throughout the ride. While the entire route is paved, much of the pavement is rough. Roads are all two-lane and shoulderless, with the exceptions of brief stretches of broad-shouldered Highway 395. Many stretches are winding and you will be sharing the road with farm equipment, trucks, and local traffic not necessarily sympathetic to bicyclists. Be especially courteous as well as cautious, and help improve the reputation of cyclists in the Colville Valley.

Start

The ride begins in Chewelah, about an hour north of Spokane on Highway 395. Find the Everett Jenne Memorial city park toward the north end of town on the corner of Park Street and Lincoln Avenue (Park is the name of Highway 395 as it passes through town.) The attractive little park straddles Chewelah Creek, and has a playground and rest rooms. Plenty of free parking is available on Lincoln Avenue across from the south end of the park.

04 MILEAGE LOG

0.0	**Head east** (away from Hwy. 395/Park St.) on Lincoln.
0.1	Gess Elementary School on your left.
0.3	Jenkins High School on your right, followed by the Barbour sports complex.
0.5	**Turn right** on Ehorn Ln. (Lincoln continues straight ahead as a dirt road.) Proceed up the hill.
0.7	**Turn left** (the only way you can turn) at the stop sign on Flowery Trail. Ehorn continues straight ahead, turning 90° into Main and taking you back downtown. Downtown Chewelah is visible on your right down the hill before you turn. After you turn, Quartzite Mountain looms in front of you. Just to the left of it, you can see the peak of taller Chewelah Mountain, the location of 49 Degrees North ski area.
1.2	**Y** in the road: Flowery Trail continues straight ahead (eventually taking you to 49 Degrees North), and Cottonwood Creek Rd. is to the right. **Take the right fork** onto Cottonwood Creek Rd. You are now proceeding along the base of Quartzite Mountain, immediately to your left. To your right are the farmlands of the Colville Valley.
2.4	Road takes a sharp bend to the left.
2.9	Road curves to the right, followed by another left-right **S**-curve.
3.3	Horseshoe Lake Rd. intersects on the left; **continue straight ahead**, winding along the base of Parker Mountain.
4.1	Vista opens up to the left; the pointed peak of oddly named Roundtop Mountain is ahead and to your left. The road continues with only the gentlest of inclines and declines.
6.0	Cross Cottonwood Creek.
6.2	**Turn right** on Hafer, a gray ribbon of road stretching straight in front of you at a moderate but steady incline for about 1-1/4 miles straight toward Wrights Mountain.
7.6	Stop-sign intersection with Highway 395. **Turn left**, exercising caution as you cross the busiest highway in this part of the state. Use the adequate right shoulder as you proceed south down this brief stretch of highway.
7.9	**Take the VALLEY/SPRINGDALE/STATE HWY. 231 exit** to your right. The winding road between here and Valley can be treacherous with respect to traffic. A pine-covered hill rises sharply to your left and the road drops off to farmland below on your right. Your route converges

with that of the Burlington Northern railroad and the tracks parallel the road for the final mile and a quarter into Valley.

11.2	ENTERING VALLEY sign.
11.3	90° left-hand bend.
11.4	90° right-hand bend.
11.5	Kimball's Kitchen restaurant is in front of you and on the left (see *Other Activities In and Around The Route*). **Turn right** on road signed WAITTS LAKE. Valley General Store (groceries, hardware, hunting and fishing licenses) is on your right after the turn.
11.6	Rough RR Crossing.
11.7	Cross Colville River. Leaving Valley, the speed limit increases to 50mph. Gravel trucks frequently speed down this route from the quarries west of Waitts Lake and seem to consider 50 the minimum. Be alert.
12.85	Intersection: Farm-to-Market Rd. to the right, Long Prairie Rd. to the left. **Continue straight** and up a steep half-mile grade.
14.25	Road forks. Left fork (Waitts Lake South Road) goes uphill sharply; **continue straight** (on the right fork).
14.4	Intersection on your left. Stay right. Sparking Waitts Lake comes into view on your left, and you enter into the densely settled but low-key resort area of the north lake shore. Use caution due to pedestrian and vehicle traffic.
14.9	Silver Beach Resort office and store on your left.
15.35	Waitts Lake Grocery on your left.
15.65	Hoag Rd. (dirt) intersects on your right as you leave the north shore resort area. Continue straight ahead and uphill briefly.
15.9	**Turn left** on Waitts Lake South Rd., keeping the lake in view on your left as you curve around the much less populated west end of the lake.
17.8	Enter the south lake shore residential area. Driveways and crossroads once again necessitate caution for the next 1/3 mile, followed by an ascent as you leave the settled area.
18.7	Begin a descent toward the Waitts Lake Rd. from which you originally accessed the lake.
18.8	*CAUTION: YIELD TO TRAFFIC* as you merge back into Waitts Lake Rd. and turn right, heading east. Enjoy the descent of the hill.
20.2	**Turn left** on Farm-to-Market Rd. at the bottom of the hill. Aptly named, Farm-to-Market winds along the west side of the farm-dotted

	Colville Valley, beginning with a flat 1-1/2 mile stretch followed by rolling hills.
22.3	Left intersection with Wrights Valley Rd. (dirt).
22.85	Gravel Newton Rd. intersects on the right, traversing the valley all the way to Hwy. 395.
25.1	Heine Rd. intersects on the left, followed immediately by a sharp bend to the right. You are now heading due east.
25.7	RR Crossing.
25.9	Stop-sign T-intersection with Hwy. 395. Exercise caution as you **turn left** on this sometimes-busy highway.
26.4	Smith Rd. intersects on the right. This is the access road to any of several Native American tribally-run casinos. Washington state law allows for "Nevada-style" gambling in limited situations where the profits accrue to the support of the tribes. **Continue straight** on 395.
27.2	Road to Browns Lake intersects on the left.
28.0	Indian Ridge Rd. and Cemetery Rd. intersect on the right.
28.1	Cross Colville River.
28.2	WELCOME TO CHEWELAH sign on the right. A PLACE FOR ALL SEASONS.
28.8	Polanski's Pizza on the left; ENTERING CHEWELAH sign on the right. Cross-traffic and commercial development.
29.25	Stop-light intersection with Main St. A right turn would take you toward 49 Degrees North ski area. The Neighbors Bakery & Deli is on the northeast corner of this intersection. **Continue straight.**
29.6	Intersection with Lincoln Ave. **Turn right**, cross over Chewelah Creek next to the park and return to the start of the ride.

Other Activities In and Around the Route Area

The Chewelah area is brimming with possibilities for the outdoor recreationist. Waitts is a trout fishing lake, with boat launching, resort, and RV facilities, and covers approximately a square mile. Nearby Jumpoff Joe Lake is also fished for trout, as are Deer and Loon lakes. The latter two have been known to yield kokanee (silver) salmon, bass, catfish and other species as well. The area is also popular with hunters. More information on fishing and hunting can be obtained from the Department of Fish and Wildlife's Spokane office at 509-456-4082 or the state headquarters at 360-902-2200

Chewelah itself is growing, and offers a selection of restaurants, lodgings and other services. The Neighbors Bakery & Deli does an excellent job with treats and sandwiches. For a char-broiled burger, a huge plate of nachos, or an epic Polanski's pizza, stop at Polanski's on the south end of town. A favorite of local sportsmen, Polanski's is a great place to enjoy a brew, a milk shake or an espresso drink while watching big-screen TV (if you're not intolerant of smoke). For lodging choices, contact the Chamber at 509-935-8991.

Kimball's Kitchen, along the route in Valley, is a local favorite spot for a solid, stick-to-your-ribs meal . The cuisine, while not original, is well-liked; there's always someone occupying some or all of the eight or nine tables. If you're up for a breakfast or lunch stop en route, it's a good bet. Espresso drinks are served.

If you can eat only one meal during your stay, don't miss Mama Monica's in Addy, just ten minutes up the highway from Chewelah. Mama Monica, who has—believe it or not—played hostess to some of Hollywood's brightest stars, has put together a restaurant that is an experience in both quality and quantity (I dare you to clean your plate). You'll be surprised at the variety of inspired offerings and the expertise of the preparation. The multi-page menu boasts—among other things—two dozen hamburgers, every breakfast item you could desire, and dinner entrees from pasta (a full page of selections) to veal to chicken. Try the Fra Diavolo Ramani, linguine in a seafood sauce featuring lobster, clams and shrimp. Mama Monica's is open 7:00am to 10:00pm daily, and dress is decidedly casual.

This bucolic farm is along Highway 231

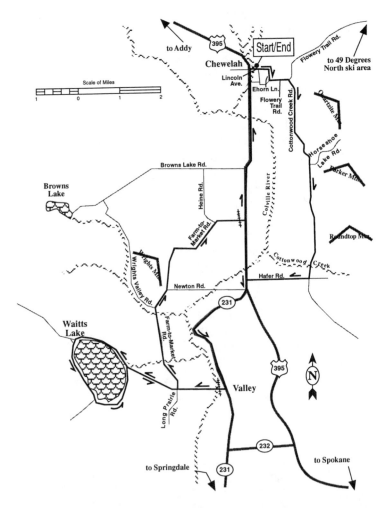

Waitts Lake-Chewelah Scenic

■ Intermediate — 29.6 miles

ᗝ **7** ᗝ
Best of Spokane Mini-Loops

● Easy Riverside Park Ride. 7.6 miles
● Easy Riverfront Park Ride. 9.2 miles
May not be suitable for children due to traffic
and one steep hill in each ride.

Highlights

Riverside ride: wooded, natural setting, Bowl and Pitcher
rock formations. Riverfront ride: historic Browne's Addition
neighborhood, Cheney Cowles Museum, Campbell House, part
of Bloomsday foot race route. Both rides: views of the Spokane
River.

General Descriptions

The Riverside ride begins at the Bowl and Pitcher Park
(named for rock formations resembling these kitchen items)
within Riverside State Park, along the northwest edge of the
city. From the park, which offers overnight camping, day
hiking, mountain bike trails and picnicking, the route follows
the Spokane River south, turns east and uphill into a residential
neighborhood, winds along a golf course, and then drops down
to river level to return through Riverside Park to Bowl and
Pitcher.

The Riverfront ride is not for speedsters, as it includes many
turns and passes through congested downtown and residential
areas. It is also inappropriate for most children, as it uses
sections of high-traffic roads, contains difficult intersections, and
has one strenuous uphill climb. It is, however, an enjoyable and
a safe ride for the moderately fit cyclist, and it includes many
fascinating aspects of Spokane. The ride begins downtown,
where you must navigate carefully through traffic to reach the
stately Browne's Addition neighborhood. There, you wind
slowly past massive historical homes and the Cheney Cowles
Museum. The remainder of the ride includes part of the scenic
City Drive route as well as part of the route of Lilac Bloomsday,
the largest timed foot race in the nation. A steep climb up Pettet
Drive (Bloomsday's "doomsday hill") puts you back into
metropolitan Spokane for the return to downtown.

Riverside Park Ride Start

Riverside State Park, located in northwest Spokane, runs along the Spokane River for several miles and is easy to find on any Spokane city map. The ride begins at Bowl and Pitcher Park, which is located within Riverside State Park, along the east side of the river. Brown and white directional signs help point the way to both Riverside and Bowl and Pitcher parks.

From the east, enter Riverside Park via Maxwell/Mission avenues and Pettet Drive; from the west, via Government Way and Fort Wright Drive. Downriver Drive becomes the Aubrey L. White Parkway a few miles south of Bowl and Pitcher, which is on your left as you head north. Bowl and Pitcher Park is open 8:00am 'til dusk, with overnight campers allowed to arrive until 10:00pm. Mileage calculation begins at the exit gate of the park.

📷 Mileage Log

0.0	**Turn right** as you leave the exit gate of Bowl and Pitcher Park, heading south on Aubrey L. White Parkway. Bicyclists are common along this route, but use caution as you share the winding route with automobiles. Some may find the lack of guardrail and the drop-off to the Spokane River on the right a bit disconcerting.
0.9	Entrance to the City of Spokane Wastewater Treatment Plant on your right (not one of the most scenic parts of the ride), followed by another mile of winding alongside the river.
2.1	Pass through the stone monument that marks the exit of the park. The other (northbound) side of the monument reads AUBREY L. WHITE PARKWAY. **Immediately following the monument, turn left,** doubling back to head south and up a 0.4 mile hill to a residential area.
2.5	Reach the top; intersection of Downriver Drive (which you have been on) and Columbia Circle. **Bear right** onto Columbia Circle. This puts the Downriver Municipal Golf Course on your right and the residential area on your left. Cora, Alice, and Euclid avenues intersect to your left as you curve around this road. The name of the road you are on changes to Riverview Drive. "Alphabet" streets intersect on your left (G, F, E, D...), and a drop-off to the river and park are on your right.
3.25	The Fort Wright Drive bridge over the Spokane River is visible ahead and to your right down in the valley below. **Turn left** (the only way you can turn) on A St. N.
3.3	Take the first **right turn**, on Grace Ave.
3.5	**Turn left** on Alberta St.

3.6	Stop-light intersection; **turn right** on Northwest Blvd.
3.7	Another stop-light intersection; **turn right** on Meenach Dr., a busier, four-lane thoroughfare. You now leave the residential neighborhood and head downhill. Stay right.
4.0	**Turn right**, taking a sort of right-hand exit ramp and following the signs for RIVERSIDE STATE PARK and DOWNRIVER DRIVE. *CAUTION!* Stop sign at bottom of this descent.
4.1	**T**-intersection with Downriver Drive; **turn right.** You are now down almost to the level of the Spokane River, which flows to your left as you re-enter Riverside Park.
5.2	Fork in the road. **Bear right**, following the most obvious road.
5.3	RIVERPARK CONVALESCENT HOME sign on the left. Only the sign remains; the facility itself was closed then destroyed in the early 1990's.
5.45	**Y**-intersection. Using caution, **take the left fork.** (The right fork is the continuation of Downriver Drive, upon which you turned to go uphill to the residential area earlier in the ride.)
5.5	Pass the stone AUBREY L. WHITE PARKWAY monument markers from which you exited earlier in the ride. Follow this road back to the ride's start, passing the wastewater treatment plant en route.
7.6	Bowl and Pitcher Park on your left; end of ride.

Riverfront Park Ride

Parking can be tricky in the congested area around Riverfront Park, located on the Spokane River just north of downtown. Park anywhere you can, then proceed to the Looff Carrousel on the south side of the park. (This beautiful carrousel is a 1909 antique with 54 hand-carved horses.) The ride begins at the Carrousel Cafe, from the little one-way drop-off drive that loops off Spokane Falls Boulevard to pass the carrousel and the cafe.

OM MILEAGE LOG

0.0	**Turn right** out of the driveway onto Spokane Falls Blvd. Immediately **work your way to the left lane** in preparation for a left turn at the second light. (Or stay right, dismount your bike and walk it across the crosswalks to effect a left turn on Post St.)
0.1	**Turn left** on Post St. Both Spokane Falls and Post are one-way streets. (Just before the turn, note the David Govedare sculpture on your right at the corner. The sculpture, entitled *The Joy of Running Together* and depicting a row of joggers, was dedicated to the Lilac

Bloomsday Festival and foot race in 1985.) As you ride through downtown, exercise caution with regard to pedestrian and vehicle traffic, open car doors, etc.

0.45 | Pass under the Amtrak/Burlington Northern railroad overpass.

0.5 | **Turn right** on 2nd Ave. Pass through several stop-light intersections on this one-way, heavily trafficked street.

1.1 | Intersection of Maple St. and 2nd Ave.; cross under another railroad overpass.

1.15 | **Y**-intersection. **Take the right fork**, continuing on the narrower road that goes essentially straight, rather than the main arterial that curves to the left. The straight fork remains 2nd Ave.; the left fork becomes Sunset Blvd. A sign on your left indicates that you are entering the Browne's Addition neighborhood.

1.35 | **Turn right** on Cannon St., following the sign to the CHENEY COWLES MUSEUM.

1.45 | **Roundabout intersection** with Pacific Ave., **continue straight** on Cannon by following the roundabout counterclockwise.

1.5 | **Turn left** on 1st Ave. W., following the signs toward CHENEY COWLES MUSEUM and CITY DRIVE.

1.7 | Entrance to parking lot of Cheney Cowles Museum on your right. To the left of the museum is the Campbell House, which offers tours giving insight into Spokane's early settlers and the history of the town. Large and stately homes grace this area, especially this block. As you pass in front of the museum, one of the grandest homes, with four massive white columns, is directly in front of you at the corner of 1st Ave. and Poplar St.

1.8 | **Turn left** on Poplar St.

1.85 | Still following the City Drive signs, **turn right** on Pacific Ave.

1.95 | **Turn left** (the only option) on Couer d'Alene.

2.2 | **Y**-intersection. **Take the right fork**, following the City Drive sign.

2.3 | 5th Ave. W. intersects on the left. **Bear right** down a short hill. *CAUTION:* Stop sign and major thoroughfare at the bottom of the hill.

2.4 | **Turn right** on Sunset Blvd. at the stop sign at the bottom of the hill. Cross Latah Creek, either with traffic or by walking your bike across the pedestrian path.

2.8 | Stop-light intersection. **Turn right** on Government Way.

3.4 | Riverside intersects to the right. Government Way continues in a long, gentle downhill slope for another 0.3 miles.

3.8	Begin "Cemetery Row." (Greenwood Memorial Terrace on your left.)
4.05	Attractive, pink stone Riverside Mausoleum on your right.
4.2	MOUNT NEBO gate entrance on the left.
4.8	**Turn right** on Fort Wright Drive, following signs for CITY DRIVE, LILAC BLOOMSDAY ROUTE, AND SPOKANE FALLS COMMUNITY COLLEGE. Go up a slight 0.2-mile hill.
5.25	First entrance to Spokane Falls Community College on your left.
5.6	Stop light marks another entrance and parking lot for the college.
5.7	Begin a downhill.
6.0	Official Bike Lane begins.
6.1	Begin crossing the Spokane River.
6.2	**Turn right**, following CITY DRIVE and RIVERSIDE PARK signs, curving around to the right in a traffic cloverleaf.
6.3	Stop sign. Riverside State Park and City Drive are to the right. **Turn left**, following Lilac Bloomsday course and Bike Route up Pettet Drive. Now *this* is a hill—a half-mile of pure hell (but such a relief when it's over!).
6.8	Top o' the hill; enter the West Central neighborhood.
7.1	Mission Ave. intersects and road begins to **curve left**; follow the curve into a 90° change in direction, exercising caution as several roads intersect here. You are now on Maxwell Ave.
7.45	Stop-light intersection with Ash St., followed immediately by another stop-light intersection with Maple St. Continue straight on Maxwell Ave.
7.6	**Y**-intersection. **Veer left**, continuing on the BIKE ROUTE. (A green Bike Route sign is visible just ahead on this left fork, which continues to be Maxwell Ave.)
7.95	Stop-light intersection. **Turn right** on Monroe St., a busy four-lane arterial that will take you directly back to Downtown and Riverfront Park.
8.6	Begin crossing the Spokane River on the ornate and historic Monroe Street Bridge. A pedestrian lane is available if you would prefer to walk your bike across this busy bridge.
8.8	**Turn left** on one-way Main Ave. *CAUTION: DIFFICULT INTERSECTION.* Several busy streets come together at this point; crosswalk is available. Proceed east on Main Ave. into the downtown Spokane

shopping district with its heralded skywalks, providing climate-controlled indoor store-to-store shopping year-round.

9.1 | **Turn left** on Howard St.

9.2 | Spokane Falls Blvd., Riverfront Park and carrousel. End of ride.

Other Activities In and Around the Route Area

Spokane is a great cycling community. Choosing a bike route in Spokane is like being a child with her head dunked in a vat of chocolate. All you can do is say, "Lord, give me the appetite to do justice to all this!" With the exception of Division Street and posted segments of Ruby and Browne, all streets are open to cyclists. Bicycling is further encouraged by many miles of signed Bike Routes. Be advised that riding on the sidewalk—never a good idea anyway—is illegal in downtown Spokane. For more information on bicycling Spokane, contact the Arrivee Cycling Club at P.O. Box 3027, Spokane 99220; The Spokane Bicycle Club at P.O. Box 62, Spokane 99210 or 509-325-1171; or the City of Spokane Bicycling Coordinator at City Hall, 2nd Floor or 509-625-6060.

The two short routes selected for this guide depart from two wonderful and contrasting parks: Riverfront (in downtown Spokane) and Riverside (along the northwest edge of Spokane). While the parks' names are confusing in their similarity, they could not be more different. Riverfront, developed for the 1974 World's Fair Expo, is a carefully crafted urban park with manicured gardens, amusement park rides and an Imax theater; Riverside is a wooded glen that takes advantage of nature's offerings. Either park offers activities sufficient for an entire day. For enjoyable family pedaling, take the kids to Riverfront Park and explore the special "wheels only" paved paths throughout this 100-acre landscaped recreation area. Mountain bike enthusiasts and day hikers will appreciate the miles of interesting trails that wind out of the Bowl and Pitcher area of Riverside Park.

Aside from cycling, Spokane offers every activity and amenity you would expect in eastern Washington's largest city. Lodgings range from budget motels and RV parks to 4-star hotels and bed and breakfasts. Restaurants of nearly every type can be found. The Spokane Opera House hosts traveling Broadway shows and is home to the Spokane Symphony Orchestra. Other performance venues include the Metropolitan

Performing Arts Center and many private clubs. Or just enjoy the admission-free beauty of Manito Park on the city's south hill, with indoor and outdoor gardens including the Gaiser Conservatory (tropical flowers and plants), the Duncan Garden (formal European-style garden), and the Japanese Garden (in honor of Spokane's sister city, Nishinomiya, Japan). For further information, contact the Spokane Convention and Visitors Bureau at 509-624-1341.

"The Joy of Running Together." This charming sculpture is in honor of the Lilac Bloomsday Race, the largest timed foot race in the nation

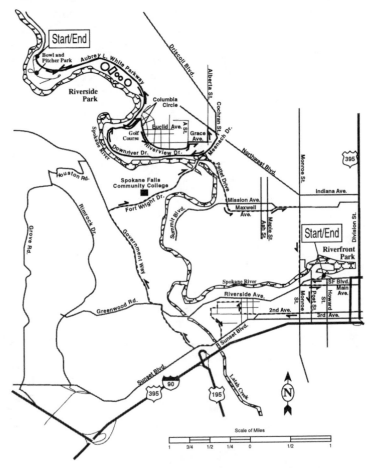

Best of Spokane Mini-Loops

● Easy, Riverside Park Ride — 7.6 miles (———)
● Easy, Riverfront Park Ride — 9.2 miles (- - - - -)

🚲 **8** 🚲
Ritzville Ride

● Easy — 11.8 miles
Mostly flat.

Highlight
Community of Ritzville, in the heart of Washington's wheat country.

Route Description
Thanks to the Ritzville Biathlon, an annual event held the first weekend in June, for helping to define this course. After exploring no fewer than a dozen routes in Ritzville, all of which ended up turning to dirt or gravel a few miles from town, I fell back on a modified version of the established biathlon route. Leave Ritzville High School, and slip out the northeast corner of town and into the fields almost immediately. A turn takes you east across the highway, after which the road curves south. A final turn takes you west, back across the highway and to the high school.

Start
Begin at the high school, at the east edge of town on Wellsandt Road. Plenty of parking is available across the street and to the east. Mileage is calculated from the horse sculpture in front of the high school.

🕐 MILEAGE LOG

0.0	From the high school, **turn right** onto Wellsandt Rd. Pass the elementary school and its driveway on your right.
0.1	**Turn right** on 6th Ave., just past the elementary school driveway and sign.
0.2	6th Ave. **curves left** into Chelan. Continue on Chelan.
0.35	Chelan goes down a short, steep hill. *CAUTION:* stop sign and main road at the bottom of the hill.
0.4	**Turn right** onto 1st Ave. at the stop-sign intersection. 1st Ave. is also Business Route 90. You are initially traveling on a two-lane road with a shoulder. As you leave town, you lose the shoulder.

1.2	Bauman Rd. intersects on the left. Continue straight ahead. The road you are on has changed to Danekas Rd.
2.4	Sage Rd. intersects on the left. Continue on Danekas Rd. Your route parallels the railroad tracks on your left.
4.1	**Y**-intersection; right fork goes to Spokane, left fork (straight ahead) to Harrington. **Take the right fork,** which curves around to the right and heads due west toward the freeway.
4.8	Crossroads before the freeway overpass. Autos can go right for I-90 West, or straight ahead for I-90 East. **Go straight,** up and over the overpass.
5.1	On the other side of the overpass, where automobiles have the opportunity to turn left to the freeway on-ramp for I-90 East, you will **go straight.**
5.5	Road makes a **90° bend to the right.** An unimproved road continues straight ahead, but you follow the obvious bend to the right.
6.5	Neergaard Rd. intersects on the left.
8.1	Yield-sign **T**-intersection with Wellsandt Rd. Marengo is to the left; Ritzville is to the right. **Turn right,** being attentive for gravel in the roadway. Watch for the Volkswagen metal "sculpture" on your left just after the turn.
8.6	Klein Rd. intersects on the left.
9.6	Benzel Rd. intersects on the left. As you approach Ritzville, you can see the freeway in front of you.
10.9	Go over the freeway overpass.
11.7	A 25-mph speed-limit sign heralds your entrance to Ritzville.
11.8	Stop sign. High school on your right; horse sculpture just ahead on the right. End of ride.

Other Activities In and Around the Route Area

Ritzville is known today primarily as a refueling stop for travelers on Interstate 90 and Highway 395, but those who stop only at the conveniently located filling stations just off the highway miss the real Ritzville. Ritzville was once the largest initial wheat shipping point in the U.S., a thriving and prosperous community in the late 19th and early 20th centuries. Vestiges of Ritzville's heyday remain in its downtown, which lies north and east of the Exit 221 services. Listed in the National Registry of Historic Places, Ritzville's downtown core contains

25 noteworthy buildings, with another 24 scattered throughout the remainder of the town. Contact the Ritzville Area Chamber of Commerce at 509-659-1936 for the brochure "Historic Ritzville: A Self-Guided Tour."

Present-day Ritzville, the Adams County seat, is home to a population of about 1800, and offers a full range of services. According to the Chamber of Commerce, Ritzville has 117 motel rooms, 56 RV hook-ups, and 11 restaurants, many of which are in the downtown core. One surprising oasis, however, sits right off the highway, behind the gas stations, Zip's Drive-In, and Perkins Family Restaurant. The Crab Creek Cookhouse and Coffee Company offers wholesome, freshly-made fare. It shares a red barn structure with Sun Prairie Gift Works, which has a tasteful, fun, and eclectic selection of merchandise. Espresso drinks are, of course, available.

The ride misses the town itself, so be sure to take in the historic downtown and perhaps stop for a picnic in the Ritzville City Park, across from the golf course. This attractive park has a swimming pool, adjacent tennis courts, and a gazebo, and is the site of most Ritzville gatherings, including its summer blues festival.

Ritzville is located at the junction of Interstate 90 with highways 395 and 261. It is 60 miles from Spokane, 46 miles from Moses Lake, and 80 miles from the Tri-Cities: Richland, Pasco, and Kennewick.

Downtown Ritzville — listed in the National Registry of Historic Places

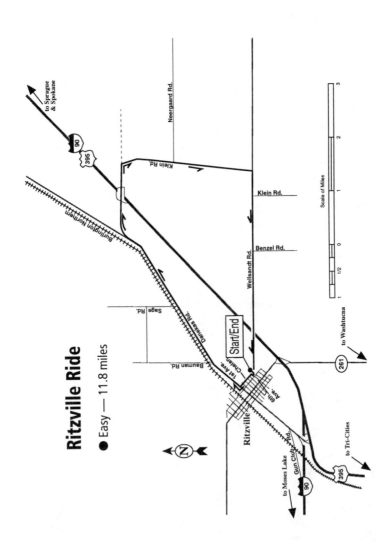

Ritzville Ride

● Easy — 11.8 miles

ᗧᗧ **9** ᗧᗧ
Palouse Tour from Colfax

■ Intermediate — 36.2 miles

Rolling hills.

Highlights

Colfax's Codger Pole and downtown corridor; pleasant rolling terrain and bucolic farmland; community of Palouse.

Route Description

This ride tours the area of rolling wheatfield hills in southeastern Washington known as The Palouse. Beginning from the quaint and historic community of Colfax, it follows rural Highway 272 East to Clear Creek Road, then loops to the village of Palouse. The return is via Highway 272, which re-joins the outbound route after about 30 miles. The roadway is generally well-paved but shoulderless, with light traffic. Rolling hills throughout the ride; scenery consists of scattered farmhouses and ranch land, with a few shady pine groves. Take water, and be attentive to traffic.

Start

Colfax is about an hour south of Spokane on Highway 195, just fifteen minutes north of Pullman, home of Washington State University. Highway 195, as it passes through town, is Main Street. Our ride begins at the Codger Pole, the largest chain-saw sculpture in the world. Located on the west side of Main, the pole is a sixty-five foot monument to an epic football rematch between the Colfax Bulldogs and the St. John Eagles, played fifty years following the original 1938 game, using the same players, cheerleaders and fans. The pole, and the good-natured brouhaha surrounding the Codger Bowl rematch, were covered by *People* magazine. While the pole area does not provide a great deal of parking, it is a charming feature of this delightful city. Park elsewhere if need be, and re-set your computer at the pole.

OH MILEAGE LOG

0.0	Begin at the Codger Pole. **Turn left** (north) on Main St. and head toward the main downtown corridor.
0.15	Stop-light intersection. **Turn right** on Canyon St., following the signs toward Palouse/East Hwy. 272. Head up a steep hill going out of town. The road is two-lane, well-paved but shoulderless, with deep drainage culverts on either side. The steepest part of the climb lasts for about 1/2 mile, then continues to climb gradually, followed by rolling hills for the balance of the ride.
1.0	Colfax Cemetery access road on the left, followed by a left-hand bend in the road, after which you can see the cemetery on your left.
1.3	Road makes a 90° bend to the right, just before Hilty Rd. intersects on the left.
4.15	North and South Palouse Grange on your right.
4.35	Schierman Rd. intersects on the left.
5.15	Begin a significant downhill through a draw timbered with ponderosa pine.
5.65	Glenwood Rd. intersects on the left.
6.0	**Y**-intersection; **take the right fork**, which is essentially straight ahead, onto Clear Creek Rd. The left fork continues to be Hwy. 272.
6.5	Cross over Clear Creek.
7.45	Enos Rd. intersects on the right.
8.1	James Rd. intersects on the left.
8.4	Group of grain storage units on the right; Stueckle Rd. intersects. Road remains flat for the next 2.4 miles.
10.8	Begin an uphill.
11.5	Top of hill—great view of the rolling Palouse hills.
14.6	Road to Kamiak Butte (Fugate Rd.) intersects on the right. The butte itself, a forested knoll 3360 ft. high, is visible on your right.
15.0	Stop-sign **T**-intersection with Hwy. 27. Historical Marker explaining Kamiak Butte is in the gravel shoulder to your right. Pullman is 9 miles to the right; Palouse is 3 miles to the left. **Turn left** on Hwy. 27.
15.9	Olson Rd. intersects on the left.
17.0	Road intersects on the right.
17.3	Self-styled antique and curiosity dealership the left. This heralds the entrance to Palouse; begin a gentle descent into town.

17.9	Entering Palouse. Note that flooding in early spring 1996 affected much of the tiny town of Palouse; locations of buildings and the precise coordinates of turns within Palouse may have changed as a result of the flooding. Basically, you will travel north through town following Hwy. 27 until you are able to head west on Hwy. 272.
18.15	*CAUTION:* Bumpy RR Crossing; road surfaces become rougher.
18.4	Cross the Palouse River; flashing-light intersection immediately following. Downtown Palouse, one of the oldest towns in the county, lay immediately to the right of this intersection before the flood of 1996. Following the flood, many of the town's historic buildings, and the downtown core itself, were being moved to higher ground. **Continue straight** on Hwy. 27 at the light. Road veers to the left and up a hill.
18.65	Follow the sign that points you **left toward Colfax** (via Hwy. 272). You will be going through a series of right-angle bends and passing through a residential as you leave town; use caution.
19.0	Road takes a 90° bend to the right and goes down a hill.
19.15	Bottom of the hill; cross 3 railroad tracks just before another 90° bend to the right.
19.3	90° bend to the left, then immediately re-cross the Palouse River. Climb uphill and out of Palouse.
23.4	Pass through a stand of pine trees.
24.4	For about a mile, the road is rough in places as you wind through a series of curves.
25.4	Lange Rd. intersects on the right and Swanson Rd. on the left. This area is known as Eden Valley.
26.95	James Rd. intersects on the left.
27.25	Brown Rd. intersects on the right.
28.6	Vantine Rd. intersects on the right. Begin a 0.5 mile uphill climb, followed by a downhill that takes you back to the ponderosa pine draw where 272 forked into Clear Creek Rd. earlier in the ride.
29.9	Mike Johnson Rd. intersects on the right.
30.4	Junction of Clear Creek Rd. and Hwy. 272. **Curve to the right**, following 272.
30.55	Glenwood Rd. intersects on the right, then you curve to the left and climb a short (about 0.5 mile), steep hill up out of the pine trees and back to the rolling Palouse.
31.8	Schierman Rd. intersects on the right.

33.1	Steep, 1/4 mile uphill.
34.8	Hilty Road intersects at a sharp angle on the right.
35.2	Cemetery access road intersects on the right.
35.5	Entering Colfax; begin a downhill grade that eventually reaches a 10% pitch on the way into Colfax. While the speed limit for vehicles is posted at 25 mph, be cautious and alert on this very steep descent.
36.05	Stop-light intersection with Main St. **Turn left** cautiously, as this four-lane is the main arterial of Colfax.
36.2	Finish at Codger Pole.

Other Activities In and Around the Route Area

Colfax is a charming community offering basic amenities and a growing array of tourist services. Both Colfax and Palouse have historic homes and buildings, including the beautifully restored 1884 Perkins House of Colfax, open to the public June-September. Call the Colfax Chamber of Commerce at 509-397-3712 for more information. Many of Palouse's historic buildings were damaged in the spring 1996 floods, but will be reconstructed.

Just a few miles east of Colfax on Highway 26 is the Palouse Empire Fairgrounds, site of events including the Colfax Jr. Rodeo (usually Memorial Day weekend), the Palouse Empire Plowing Bee (in April), and the all-county Palouse Empire Fair (1st weekend after Labor Day).

Pullman, about 15 miles south of either Colfax or Palouse, is home to Washington State University. As such, it is the largest town in the area, with the expected accouterments of a mid-sized university town. Originally called "Three Forks," Pullman is a hilly town situated at the confluence of two creeks and the Palouse River. For current information on arts or sporting events at the college, phone 509-335-3564. Pullman's Chamber of Commerce can be reached at 1-800-365-6948 or 509-334-3565.

A bit farther afield, but absolutely worth the sixty-five mile drive, is Palouse Falls. Take Highway 26 East to Washtucna, then Highway 261 South to the Palouse Falls State Park cutoff. A two-mile gravel road takes you to the park, where the falls, a surprising oasis in the midst of the desert, plummet almost 200 feet to the solid rock gorge below. The park also offers hiking trails, restrooms and seasonal overnight camping. An excellent picnic spot. Return the same way or by taking 261 South past

Lyons Ferry State Park to Highway 12 East, then 127 North to 26. Take 26 East back into Colfax.

Codger Pole, the largest chainsaw sculpture in the world

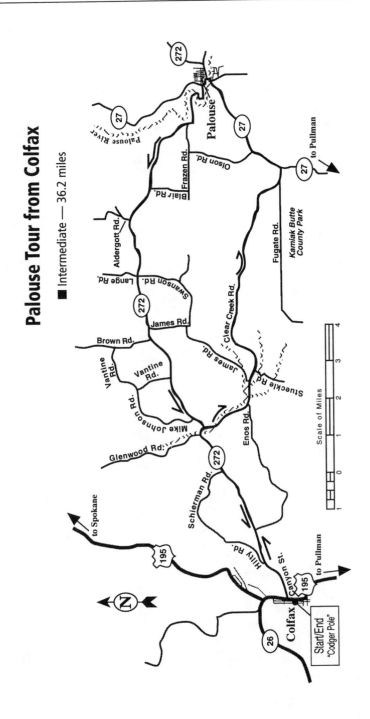

Palouse Tour from Colfax

■ Intermediate — 36.2 miles

🚴 **10** 🚴
Selah-Naches Valley

■ Intermediate — 27.2 miles

Flat to slightly rolling.

Highlights

Varied scenery and pleasant, easy cycling. Town of Selah.

General Description

This ride takes you from the community of Selah northeast into the sagebrush desert and cattle country of the Wenas Creek Valley. Follow a mostly flat, well-paved, two-lane road with views of the Cascade Mountain foothills. Turning southwest toward the town of Naches, you reach the ride's only screaming downhill at 12-1/2 miles. Just outside of Naches (where you can make an optional pit stop), turn back southeast toward Selah. This scenic part of the ride winds through dense orchards and is slightly more rolling. Be sure to bring plenty of water, as refueling opportunities are few and far between.

Start

The ride begins in Selah, just north of Yakima. If you approach Selah from Yakima, travel north on Interstate 82/Highway 12/Highway 97, then stay on 82/97 toward Ellensburg when Highway 12 forks off toward Naches and White Pass. Cross the twin bridges over the Yakima and Naches rivers' confluence, then follow the signs for 823/Selah. If traveling south on 82/97, take any Selah exit before you reach Yakima.

First Street and Wenas Road are the main north-south arterials through Selah. (Highway 823 is First Street in the south part of town, then jogs east and continues north as Wenas Rd.) Find the high school at the north end of town on the corner of First and E. Goodlander. Behind and downhill from the high school is Carlon Park. Begin the ride at the corner of E. Goodlander and Lancaster, at the exit from the Carlon Park parking lot.

[0⁴] MILEAGE LOG

0.0	**Turn right** on E. Goodlander.
0.15	Stop-light intersection with Wenas Rd. **Turn left.** This road is four-lane, well-paved, with moderate traffic.
0.6	Road forks. Right fork is continuation of 823 (Harrison Rd). **Stay left** on Wenas Rd. Road narrows to two lanes, with paved shoulder. You are leaving the town of Selah behind and entering a rural area.
1.9	Shoulder ends.
2.3	Fork in the road; Brathodve goes off to the right. Continue on the main road.
2.9	**Turn left** on Hexon Rd. To the right is Graber Rd.
3.4	Stop-sign intersection with Gore Rd. to the left and S. Wenas Rd. to the right. **Turn right** on S. Wenas Rd.
3.6	S. Wenas Rd. makes a sharp bend to the left.
4.2	Tibbling Rd. intersects on the left. S. Wenas Rd. curves off to the right and slightly downhill. You are looking down into the Wenas Valley, bordered at the north (to your right) by Umtanum Ridge. As you wind northwest through the valley, Wenas Creek flows about a half mile off to your right, roughly parallel with the road. Cleman Mountain and the Oak Creek Wildlife Area are straight ahead in the distance.
8.2	Fletcher Ln. intersects on the right.
10.1	Road bends to the left.
10.3	S. Wenas Rd. goes off to the right; **continue straight ahead** on Wye Rd. You are now heading southwest.
12.6	Exercise caution as you begin a steep, winding descent toward Naches. Road is shoulderless, with tight corners. Nice view of the Naches Valley.
13.3	Go underneath an irrigation canal overpass.
13.4	Cleman Rd. intersects from behind and on the right in a sort of reverse **Y**. The road you are on is now called Naches-Wenas Rd.
13.6	Naches-Wenas Rd. intersects with Old Naches Hwy. The community of Naches lies to the right, Old Naches Hwy. goes off to the left, and Allan Rd. continues straight ahead. **Turn left** on Old Naches Hwy. (Or, stop your mileage computer and turn right into Naches for a break, then restart your computer at this intersection. If you choose the Naches detour, don't miss the fudge factory and store on the west side of Hwy. 12 in Naches.)

13.65	Cross over a canal. (Canals not pictured on map.)
14.4	Cross canal again. You are heading southeast through the Upper Naches Valley, an orchard area. Watch for cross traffic, especially during harvest periods.
15.75	Locust Ln. intersects on the right.
16.3	Road becomes narrow with tight, winding curves, and angles uphill for about a mile.
16.7	Pass over a bridge where canals come together to join a power house on your right.
18.3	Valley View Rd. intersects on the left. Roads begin to intersect more frequently; only major navigational points are noted below.
19.8	Intersection: Pleasant Valley Rd. goes off to the left and N. Gleed Rd. to the right. Pavement improves.
20.1	Naches Valley Primary School on the right. E. Gleed merges on the right; the Lower Naches Community Park is in the V formed by the two roads as they come together.
21.4	Y-intersection. **Take the right-hand fork and curve right** onto Old Stage Way.
22.0	**Turn left** on Mapleway Rd.
22.7	N. Galloway Dr. intersects. Road begins a short uphill.
23.35	Top of the climb. Intersection with Selah Heights Rd.
23.6	Intersection. Dirt roads Slade and Brigit go forward and to the left, respectively. **Turn right**, continuing on Mapleway Rd.
24.1	Following the sign toward Selah, **turn left** on Crusher Canyon Rd.
24.4	Slade Rd. intersects on the left; Crusher Canyon Rd. bends toward the left and begins to descend into Selah.
25.1	WELCOME TO SELAH monument sign.
25.8	Lince Intermediate School on the right. At this point, the road becomes Naches Ave. **Continue straight ahead** on Naches Ave., crossing Third and Second streets.
26.0	Stop-light intersection of Naches Ave. and First. **Continue straight ahead.** You are now in downtown Selah; use caution and be alert for cross traffic.
26.1	**Turn left** on Wenas Rd., which is also North 823, a well-paved, four-lane thoroughfare.

26.3	Pass the Larson Fruit Company warehouse on your right. The high school behind which we began our ride is now visible uphill on the left.
27.0	Stop-light intersection with E. Goodlander. **Turn left.**
27.2	**Turn left** into the Carlon Park parking lot.

Other Activities In and Around the Route Area

"Selah" is a biblical word meaning "pause and meditation," and has also been compared to a Native American expression for "calm and peaceful." That is a good description of this self-contained community of 5450 residents just north of Yakima. For more information on Selah, contact its Chamber of Commerce at 509-697-5545 or City Hall at 509-698-7328.

Nearby Yakima is a multi-faceted town with a rich heritage and a full complement of modern amenities. Restaurants and lodgings are plentiful. Museums include the Yakima Electric Railway Museum, the Central Washington Agricultural Museum, and the Yakima Valley Museum, which includes a collection of over 70 horse-drawn vehicles. The Yakima Chamber of Commerce (509-248-2021) is a source for additional information including a brochure describing a pair of historical walking tours.

Beer and ale fans should visit Grant's Pub and Brewery in Yakima. Local brewmeister Bert Grant is credited with launching the microbrew industry when he expanded his home brew to a commercial scale in 1981 and founded what has become the Yakima Brewing & Malting Company. His first brew, Grant's Scottish Ale, has been joined by seven others, including Grants Pale Ale, Grant's Perfect Porter, and Grant's Imperial Stout. Grant's Pub is located in half of an old train station at 32 N. Front Street (between Yakima Avenue and B Street). The Pub offers British style fare and homemade soups and sandwiches along with the brews, and hosts regular musical events (509-575-2922). It is a non-smoking facility. The Brewery is located off W. Washington between South 3rd and South 1st/Business 97, just east of the main Yakima post office. Tours are offered by appointment (509-575-1900). Yakima Brewing & Malting Company was purchased by Stimson-Lane in late 1995, but promises to continue its tradition of no-compromise craft brewing.

While in the Yakima Valley, enjoy a bike ride along the Yakima Greenway path, a 10-mile, 3600-acre land trust along the Yakima River from Selah Gap to Union Gap dedicated to conservation and recreation. The Greenway is not part of any city or county park system, but has been developed and is maintained by the non-profit Yakima Greenway Foundation (509-453-8280). No motor vehicles are allowed (except motor-assisted wheelchairs) along the path, and the Greenway is open 6am to 9pm during daylight savings time and 7:30am to 5pm during standard time. For an easy 13.8 mile ride, begin at Harlan Landing (take Interstate 82 north of Yakima to the Resthaven Road exit, then turn west over the freeway to the parking lot) and head south until the path ends near Valley Mall Boulevard (6.9 miles); return to Harlan landing. Note that the Yakima Greenway has plans for a 3-mile extension in 1996. From the existing north point at Harlan Landing, the path will extend west along the Naches River and Highway 12 to Myron Lake, for total Greenway of about 10 miles.

A peaceful, tree-lined road just outside of Selah beckons to cyclists

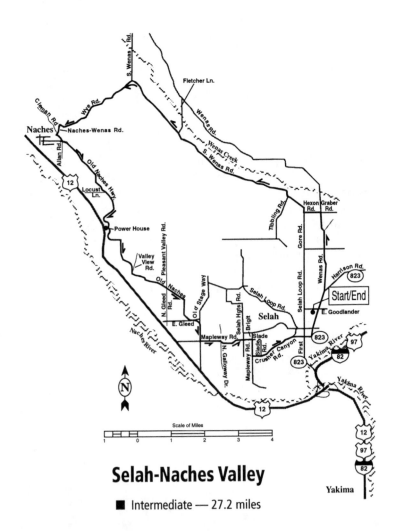

Selah-Naches Valley

■ Intermediate — 27.2 miles

ॐ **11** ॐ
Yakima Valley Wineries

● Easy — 18.0 miles

Gently rolling.

Highlights

Five wineries (Covey Run, Hyatt, Wineglass, Bonair, Zillah Oakes) and vineyard/orchard scenery.

General Description

Designed to showcase the Yakima Valley, Washington state's oldest viticultural appellation, this easy, slightly rolling ride is a relaxed and scenic introduction to Washington's thriving wine industry. It leaves the community of Zillah and loops through vineyards and orchards to visit five wineries. Pavement ranges from good to fair (patchy and chip-sealed), with two winery access roads that are hard-packed dirt/gravel, but quite navigable.

Start

The ride begins and ends in Zillah. Take Exit 52 or 54 off Interstate 82, following the signs into Zillah. You will be on First Avenue, Zillah's main street. Parking is available on the south side of First between 6th and 7th streets, or on the one-way (westbound) street immediately south of and parallel to First.

0⁴ MILEAGE LOG

0.0 | Begin at the corner of First Ave. and 6th St. **Head north** (uphill) on 6th St.

0.1 | Stop sign. **Turn right** on Second Ave. Head east through residential Zillah, climbing slightly. Pavement is patchy; watch for cross-traffic.

0.85 | Zillah High School on your right, heralding the end of town. Pavement changes to chip-sealed texture for the next 1/4 mile. Road name changes to E. Zillah Dr.

1.1 | Stop-sign intersection with Yakima Valley Highway. **Continue straight** on E. Zillah Dr., rolling into your first 1/4 mile downhill, followed by a 1/4 mile uphill, characteristic of the rollers throughout the ride. You are surrounded by vineyards and orchards as you leave town on this two-lane, shoulderless, well-paved road.

1.6 | Lucy Ln. intersects to the right, followed immediately by a crossing of Sunnyside Canal, a critical irrigation source for the wine region.

1.7 | **Turn left** on Lucy Ln., a well-paved and shoulderless road through mature orchards.

2.7 | Unmarked road intersects in both directions.

3.2 | Glacier Rd. intersects from the right.

3.7 | Stop-sign **T**-intersection with Highland Dr. **Turn left.**

4.25 | **Turn right** on Vintage Rd. This well-paved spur road takes you to your first winery.

4.8 | Hawkins Rd. intersects on the left.

5.8 | Triple-pronged **Y**-intersection. Extreme right hand fork is a dirt and gravel road that drops down into the vineyard. An unimproved road goes ahead and to the right, marked END OF COUNTY ROAD. **Take the left fork**, which is the most obvious and the only paved fork, up an incline to Covey Run.

5.95 | Covey Run parking lot. This winery, originally named Quail Run, lost its name in a dispute with a California winery of the same name. It is one of Washington's most established and respected vintners. Tasting room is open daily, 10am to 5pm April through November, and 11am to 4:30pm December through March. View cellar operations through windows. 509-829-6235. After visiting the winery, return down the hill, and turn right at the bottom to head south on Vintage Rd. the way you came in.

7.1 | Hawkins Road intersects to the right.

7.6 | **T**-intersection with Highland Dr. **Turn right.** Travel through young orchards as you head west.

8.1 | Hawkins Rd. (an L-shaped road) intersects on the right.

8.6 | **Turn right** on Roza Dr.

9.65 | **Turn left** on Gilbert Rd.

10.2 | Cheyne Rd. intersects, shortly after which you can see the red-roofed Hyatt Vineyards facility off to your left across the field.

10.7 | **Turn left** on a packed dirt and gravel road to access the winery. The entry drive takes you past labeled plantings of white riesling, merlot and chardonnay grapes.

10.85	Arrive at Hyatt Vineyards winery, a friendly barn-shaped structure situated amidst 101 acres of grapes. Enjoy tastings that may include chardonnay, merlot and cabernet plus the sweeter late harvest riesling, black muscat and ice wines. Facilities include a picnic area and a retail gift shop. Open daily 11am to 5pm (11am to 4:30pm in winter, closed in January). 509-829-6333. Leave the same way you came in.
11.0	Intersection of Hyatt access road and Gilbert Rd. **Turn left** on Gilbert Rd.
11.5	**Turn left,** following the sign for Bonair Winery. This road, which may be unmarked but is named "N. Bonair Rd.," is chip-sealed, therefore somewhat rough.
12.0	Darby Rd. (gravel) intersects on the right.
12.25	Wineglass Cellars is on the right. This winery opened in the fall of 1995; tastings available. Call for current information. 509-829-3011.
12.5	Stop-sign intersection with Highland Dr. To reach the fourth winery, **proceed straight ahead** on S. Bonair Rd. Surface is rolling, hard-packed dirt. Use caution. This is the longest dirt road on the route—a beautiful, if bumpy, 1/2-mile ride through mature orchards.
13.05	Stop your mileage computer at the gate of the Bonair Winery. Enjoy their picnic grounds, which include a pond and waterfall. Bonair has been producing Washington wines since 1985. Their fine offerings include cabernets, chardonnays, a dry riesling, a Johannisberg riesling, and several light wines. 509-829-6027. Tasting room is open daily 10am to 5pm (10am to 4:30pm, weekends only, in winter). Leave the winery the same way you came in, re-starting your computer at the gate.
13.55	**Turn right** on Highland Dr.; return to pavement.
13.8	N. Manuel Ln. intersects in both directions.
14.6	**Turn right** (south) on Cheyne Rd.
15.6	Stop-sign intersection with Yakima Valley Highway. **Continue straight** on Cheyne Rd. into the west edge of Zillah.
16.1	Zillah Middle School on your right.
16.5	Stop-sign intersection with First St.; Cherry Patch convenience store and gas station on your left. Downtown Zillah is to your left down First Ave. **Turn right** for a spur route to one final winery. Large fruit-packing facility on your right as you head down the grade. Note that Interstate 82 is just ahead; use caution and watch for automobile traffic going on and off the freeway.

16.7 | **Turn right** just before the freeway on Vintage Valley Pkwy. This newer development is designed to take advantage of freeway traffic, and offers such eye-catching fare as a Subway sandwich shop, Vintage Valley Grill, the Rocky Mountain Chocolate Factory, gas stations, convenience stores and, of course, espresso stands.

17.0 | Entrance to Zillah Oakes Winery on the right. Stop your computer. Wines available for tasting may include semillon (a popular Washington white), chardonnay, rieslings, muscat canelli, and Zillah Oakes' own Maywine. Hours 10am to 5pm daily, 11am to 4:30pm Mon.-Sat. in winter. 509-829-6990. Return the same way you came in, out Vintage Valley Pkwy.

17.2 | Stop sign. **Turn left,** going back up the hill, curving to the right toward Zillah. Again, watch for traffic exiting freeway.

17.4 | Back at the Cheyne Rd. intersection. Cherry Patch convenience store on your left, cemetery on your right. **Continue straight,** curving to the right to go back into Zillah.

18.0 | Downtown Zillah. End of ride at corner of Sixth St. and First Ave.

Other Activities In and Around the Route Area

Just south of the ride's starting point, at the corner of 7th Street and Railroad, is the Grapevine Catering & Coffee Company, an excellent lunch spot and coffee house (509-829-5533). The proprietor offers three fresh choices daily, including a fruit salad in the summer. Winter fare tends toward soups and hearty breads. Box lunches are prepared upon request, and make an excellent picnic for your winery tour. For more information on dining and lodging, contact the Zillah Chamber of Commerce at 509-829-5055.

Those new to Washington state wines and winery touring will be pleasantly surprised by the Yakima Valley. The atmosphere at most tasting rooms is laid-back, but there's nothing casual about the winemaking. The superb wines of the Yakima, Columbia, and Walla Walla appellations have been compared to the finest French wines, showing both the painstaking efforts of master vintners and the excellent suitability of these areas' water and soil for viticulture. As a bonus to the tourist, tasting rooms are especially thick along the I-82 corridor. Pick up a brochure or two at any of the wineries and visit a few more within easy driving or cycling distance.

Nearby Toppenish is a fun place to spend an afternoon. The self-described "City of Murals" displays over two dozen hand-painted scenes, part of an award-winning project sponsored by the Toppenish Mural Society (509-865-6516). The downtown is restored with an "Old West" theme, and includes a variety of gift and antique shops. This tourist-friendly town has a festival of some sort just about every month, including the "Mural-In-A-Day" in June, during which a new mural is added to the town's collection, painted by a cadre of artists in one day as the curious look on. Toppenish's Chamber of Commerce can be reached at 509-865-3262.

A must-see attraction in Toppenish is the Yakima Nation Cultural Center, on Highway 97 southwest of town (509-865-2800). It is easy to spot with its peaked roof imitating the shape of Native American dwellings. The museum has a well-presented collection of Yakima (also spelled "Yakama") artifacts and provides an important historical perspective. With a restaurant, gift shop, and theater inside, the Cultural Center provides an entertaining outing for all ages.

Less well-known is the American Hop Museum, located at the corner of Satus Avenue and South B Street. Obscure? Perhaps. But, in addition to the celebrated wine grapes, Yakima Valley produces nearly *three-fourths* of our nation's hops. Learn more at this interesting little museum.

The American Hop Museum. Nearly three-fourths of the country's hops are grown in the Yakima Valley.

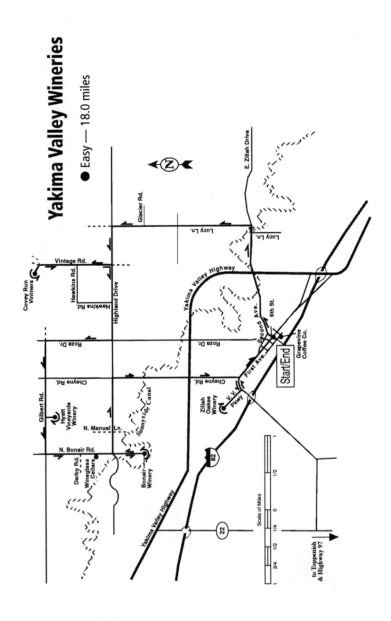

Yakima Valley Wineries

● Easy — 18.0 miles

ᗝᕗ **12** ᗝᕗ
Richland-Benton City Loop

■ Intermediate — 31.5 miles

Gentle hills.

Highlights

Oakwood Cellars winery, Yakima and Columbia River scenery, Bear Hut homestyle restaurant at halfway point, Green Gage Plum Cafe and Espresso near ride's end.

General Description

This ride begins in Richland, home of the U.S. Department of Energy's Hanford site, notable for its historic role in our nation's defense, and current workplace of thousands of research scientists, engineers, and environmental science technicians. The route utilizes excellent paved surfaces over a series of rolling hills through farmland and rural residential areas, includes a spur into Benton City for a café stop, and then follows the Yakima River past a winery. The return is flat and scenic, reaching Richland via the community of West Richland.

Start

Begin at Howard Amon Park in Richland, at the far east end of Lee Boulevard. The 46-acre park, named for an orchardist and founding father of Richland, is flanked by the mighty Columbia River. Facilities include boat launches, tennis courts, public restrooms, picnic/barbecue areas, playground equipment, a children's wading pool, and the architecturally unique Ellipsoid performance stage. Ample parking is available in a lot off Lee Blvd. and behind the Ellipsoid stage.

0⋮ MILEAGE LOG

0.0	From Howard Amon Park, head west on Lee Blvd., up a slight grade.
0.1	**Proceed straight** through the stoplight at George Washington Way; stay in the left lane.
0.2	**Turn left** at the Jadwin Ave. stoplight.
0.3	**Stay right** (essentially straight ahead) as Jadwin Ave. forks.

Jadwin Ave. takes you through the residential area of south Richland, past Lewis & Clark Elementary School (on your left at 1/2 mile).

1.1   At the second stop sign (Abbot St.), the road ahead is a dead end for automobiles. A pedestrian/bicycle access allows you to **proceed straight ahead**, through the trees, between two sets of metal uprights and **continue straight** on Jadwin Ave. through a residential apartment complex.

1.2   The next stop sign is Aaron Dr., at which you **turn right**. Proceed on Aaron Dr. past commercial development (quick marts, fast food, a shopping center) and up a hill that curves to the left to the intersection of Hwy. 240 and Interstate 182 at a stoplight at the top of the hill.

1.8   **Continue straight ahead and enter the freeway (I-182)**, using extreme caution due to merging traffic on the right. A generous shoulder is provided through this short section of highway, which takes you across the Yakima River.

2.4   Immediately following the Yakima River bridge, you will **take Exit 3**, KENNEDY ROAD/COLUMBIA DRIVE. **Stay right.**

2.6   **Turn right** at the stop sign at the top of the exit ramp. Follow an **S-**curve series. You are now on Kennedy Rd., a two-lane highway through sagebrush desert on which you will stay for the next several miles. As the road straightens to parallel Interstate 82 (visible on your left), you see Candy Mountain directly in front of you; to its right is Red Mountain. To your left stretches the elongated bulk of Badger Mountain. To the right of Red Mountain you can see Rattlesnake Mountain, the tallest treeless mountain in North America (it looks small from this vantage point, but note its size as you continue along the route).

4.0   Caution: narrow bridge; shoulder disappears temporarily. With the exception of this short bridge, Kennedy Rd. has ample shoulder, as well as an excellent paved surface and very light traffic. You will experience a continuous but gentle incline for several miles.

4.7   Opportunity for a shorter route cutoff. (Those desiring a shorter ride may turn right on Bombing Range Rd., which takes you up a rather challenging hill and over to the city of West Richland. Bombing Range Rd. ends on Van Giesen St. and a right turn here heads you back toward Richland.)

5.25   As you continue on Kennedy Rd., past cattle and other farm lands, you begin the ride's steepest incline.

7.0	The ridges of the Horse Heaven Hills mesas are now visible in front of you. Wild horses have roamed and are said to still roam this vast plateau, which stretches for thousands of acres to the Oregon border.
10.0	Begin the gradual descent into Benton City. *CAUTION: STOP SIGN NEAR BOTTOM OF DESCENT!*
11.2	Kennedy Rd. terminates at a stop-sign intersection with Hwy. 224. **Proceed straight (downhill)** onto Hwy. 224 West. (The measured route includes a spur into Benton City and back; if you wish to skip this spur, you may turn right at this stop sign and head east on Hwy. 224, turning left onto Demoss Road. Subtract 3.2 miles from overall ride length.)
11.4	At the bottom of the hill on Hwy. 224 West, you will **turn right** and cross the bridge over the Yakima River into Benton City. Remain on this street (Hwy. 225 North) as it winds into downtown Benton City and becomes, in effect, its main street.
12.6	"Downtown" Benton City, where you will find a cash machine, produce stand, hardware store, convenience store, and a couple of dining opportunities.
12.8	The Bear Hut family restaurant, locally famous for stellar flapjacks and enormous home-style sandwiches. This, the corner of Della and Ninth streets, marks the **turnaround point**. Leave Benton City the same way you came in.
14.2	Again cross the Yakima River bridge (this stretch of the Yakima is idyllic for canoeing), then **turn left** back up the hill onto Hwy. 224 East.
14.4	You will see a blue TOURIST INFORMATION sign indicating three wineries ahead and to the left. Follow this sign, **veering left** at the top of the rise rather than going straight and back onto Kennedy Rd. This brief grade has very little shoulder, but traffic is light. Watch for the intersection sign for DEMOSS ROAD, and the TOURIST INFORMATION sign for OAKWOOD CELLARS.
14.9	Make the **left turn** onto Demoss Rd. and follow its picturesque route along the orchard- and vineyard-lined banks of the Yakima River.
15.8	You may wish to stop at Oakwood Cellars winery at 2321 Demoss Rd. (509-588-5332). Demoss Rd. continues through farmland, passing Songbird Island on the left and occasional basalt formations rising to your right.
18.9	The road forks, and you will continue **straight ahead (on the right fork)**; the route becomes Ruppert Rd. and heads back toward Richland and West Richland at a slight incline. As you approach West

Richland, the lack of zoning results in an interesting hodgepodge of buildings including in-home antique stores and produce stands in season. At this point, the ridge of Red Mountain looms lengthwise on your right. When the road turns northeast (with Red Mountain at your back), you will be facing the geological formation known as White Bluffs, which is the east bank of the Columbia River in the distance some nine or ten miles away.

24.2	Ruppert Rd. terminates on Hwy. 224; **turn left** and proceed into West Richland.
25.8	Bombing Range Rd. intersects Hwy. 224 (which is also known as Van Giesen St. at this point); this is the point where the short route cutoff joins the main route.
26.4	The Green Gage Plum Cafe & Espresso on your left is noteworthy for a limited menu of tasty and wholesome fare. Basic services such as convenience stores are also nearby.
26.5	West Richland's only full-service grocery store, Mel's Food Center, is on your left.
26.6	You will again cross the Yakima River, where the town's rural heritage is indicated by the sign that says "Dismount and Lead Horses." Whatever species of livestock you might have missed in Benton City are likely present on this final leg through West Richland.
28.2	Intersection of Van Giesen St./Hwy. 224 and Hwy. 240. Approach with caution; you should be in the **center lane** when you reach the light. Proceed **straight** through and continue on Van Giesen St. into and through Richland.
29.9	Van Giesen St. turns into Hains Ave. at the intersection with Hunt Ave. Proceed on Hains Ave. up a short rise and to the right.
30.0	**Turn left** up toward a public parking lot.
30.1	At the top of the rise, **turn right** onto an asphalt bike path that parallels the Columbia River heading south.
31.5	End of ride, back at the Howard Amon Park parking lot.

Other Activities In and Around the Route Area

Richland, Pasco and Kennewick, known as the "Tri-Cities," sit at the confluence of the Columbia, Yakima and Snake rivers, thus offering a wide variety of water sport opportunities.

The main commercial district, Columbia Center, lies at the west end of Kennewick and includes a shopping mall, sports/performing arts coliseum, and a wide variety of retail shops, restaurants and lodgings. For a quiet stay close to the start of the route, try the Red Lion/Hanford House or the Shilo Inn in Richland.

A few blocks north of the ride's start is Richland's Uptown Shopping Center, a block-long outdoor mall on Jadwin Avenue and George Washington Way between Williams Boulevard and Symons Street. Cyclists will enjoy the many varieties of fresh-baked bagels—from plain or whole wheat to sun-dried tomato, jalapeño, or pesto—at Some Bagels, open 6am 'til 5pm weekdays and 7:30am 'til 3pm weekends. Some Bagels also offers sandwiches and espresso drinks. Other favorite stops at the Uptown include the eclectic Octopus' Garden gift and card shop and The Book Place, which features an incredibly diverse collection of classic and contemporary books.

Also worth a stop in Richland is Pasta Mama's (509-946-4142), a local success story with pasta and sauce factory and retail gift shop at 1270 Lee Blvd. Store hours are 10am to 6pm Mon. through Fri., 11am to 4pm Sat.

Beer aficionados will appreciate Baron's Beef & Brew, at 1034 Lee Boulevard (509-946-5500). Baron's boasts over 100 varieties of domestic and imported beer (13 on draught) as well as full lunch and dinner menus. Hours basically are 11am to 11pm, but it closes earlier Sun. and Mon., and stays open later on Fri. and following local sporting events.

No visit to Richland would be complete without a stop at CREHST: Columbia River Exhibition of History, Science & Technology. CREHST is a relatively new project, stemming from the former Hanford Museum/Hanford Science Center. While the science center had for years been a tribute to Richland's scientific heritage, housing fascinating, hands-on displays emphasizing the nuclear industry, CREHST includes information about the entire Columbia Basin, from science to agriculture to transportation. The museum, located west of the Richland Community Center off George Washington Way (509-376-6374), is open 8am to 5pm Mon. through Fri. and 9am to 5pm on Sat., and is appropriate for all ages.

In addition to Oakwood Cellars, Benton City is home to three other wineries, all of which are located on Sunset Road just off Highway 224: Kiona Vineyards Winery (509-588-6716), Seth Ryan Winery (509-588-6780), and Blackwood Canyon Vineyard (509-588-6249). Hours vary seasonally.

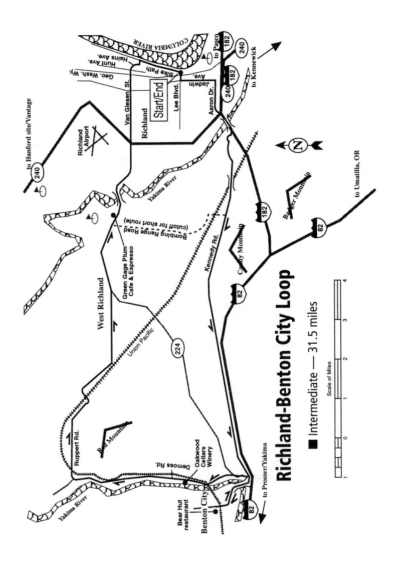

Richland-Benton City Loop

■ Intermediate — 31.5 miles

ᘓᘓ **13** ᘓᘓ
Walla Walla Stateline Loop

● Easy — 17.4 miles

Gently rolling.

Highlights
Fort Walla Walla historic complex, peaceful farm scenery, crossing into Oregon.

Route Description
From the historic Fort Walla Walla Park complex, leave the city of Walla Walla and ride into idyllic farms and fields. Heading south, you pass into Oregon and roll along good pavement up and down gentle hills through one of the northwest's premiere agricultural areas. Cross back into Washington and pedal back through the attractive community of Walla Walla before returning to the Fort on a paved recreation path.

Although the ride is not long, be sure to pack extra water if you are traveling in the heat of July or August.

Start
Mileage calculations begin at the entrance to Fort Walla Walla Park. The fort, park and campground (see *Other Activities*) are on the west side of Walla Walla, between Walla Walla and College Place. Access the park by turning north off Highway 125 onto Myra Rd., or south off Rose St. West at the Blue Mountain Mall.

🖳 MILEAGE LOG

0.0	Leaving the park, **turn left** on Myra Rd. Follow Myra Rd. slightly uphill to the intersection of Dalles Military Rd.
0.2	**Turn right** on Dalles Military Rd., a wide, two-lane, well-surfaced road with an extra-wide shoulder on the westbound side.
1.0	**Turn left** on SE Larch Ave. Proceed downhill to intersect with Hwy. 125.
1.35	Stop-sign intersection with Hwy. 125. Proceed straight across the highway.

1.4	Immediately after crossing the highway, you will come to a **T**-intersection. **Turn right** on the road marked Taumarson Rd., which becomes Dalles Military Rd. Follow this road southwest, roughly paralleling Hwy. 125, as you leave the suburbs and enter the rich agricultural basin of Walla Walla County.
1.9	**Y**-intersection. **Take the left (and most obvious) fork.** Continue as the road narrows, loses its shoulder, and winds downhill past bucolic farms and over Yellowhawk Creek.
2.15	Stop sign at S. Ninth St. **Continue straight ahead.** Road becomes Pepper Bridge Rd.
2.4	First uphill grade; begin rolling hills. Proceed through open wheatfields and ranchland.
3.65	Cross a branch of the Walla Walla River.
3.8	At the top of a short hill, you reach the Oregon state border at a **T**-intersection with Stateline Rd. **Turn left.**
3.85	Almost immediately, the **road bends right**, becoming Tum-A-Lum. Pavement quality deteriorates somewhat, and shoulders are non-existent, but traffic is very light and the scenery is lovely.
4.9	Green UMATILLA COUNTY 1 mile marker on the right-hand side of the road.
5.3	Old Tum-A-Lum school house on the left; Ferndale Rd. intersects on the right. The school house was purchased in recent years by local growers who have turned it into a processing and canning facility for gourmet specialties.
5.6	**Turn left** on Birch Creek Rd.
5.8	Cross bridge over Walla Walla River, pass through a glen with a few farm houses.
5.9	Follow road as it **curves right.**
6.0	**Curve left** at a **Y** to stay on Birch Creek Rd. For the next few miles, you will be back in open, rolling wheatfields and will basically take the turns that keep you on the paved road.
6.4	**Turn left** on Telephone Pole Rd.
6.5	**Turn right** on Birch Creek Rd. Large grain elevator looms ahead on your right. Sprawling all along the horizon are the Blue Mountains and the Umatilla National Forest.
7.7	RR crossing.

9.1	**Turn left** on unmarked but obvious Power Line Rd. A sign indicates WALLA WALLA - 7 to your left and WALLA WALLA RIVER, MILTON-FREEWATER, and other points south to your right on a less-improved road.
9.5	Cross Birch Creek.
10.8	Pass back into Washington as Stateline Rd. intersects on your left. You can now see Walla Walla ahead to the northwest.
12.1	Cross Cottonwood Creek, then enter a speed zone, heralding the outskirts of Walla Walla.
12.6	**Y**-intersection. **Take the left fork** onto Cottonwood Rd., a gentle, well-maintained downhill into Walla Walla. You are now surrounded by a few older farmhouses amongst largely newer, moderately affluent homes.
13.7	Cross Yellowhawk Creek.
13.8	4-way stop at Reser Rd. As you **continue straight,** you are now on Howard. The road widens and a BIKE ROUTE lane begins. Prospect Point Elementary on the right; Mountain View Cemetery on the left.
14.2	CITY LIMITS sign. Large, manicured Howard Tietan Park on your right.
14.45	Stop-light intersection with Tietan St. **Continue straight.** Continue on BIKE ROUTE for about 3/4 mile through established neighborhoods.
15.0	**Turn left** on E. Chestnut. Proceed through two stop lights (at 2nd Avenue and Ninth Avenue).
16.1	At the Ninth Ave. (which is also Hwy. 125) crossing, use caution. This is a major thoroughfare. E. Chestnut becomes W. Chestnut at this crossing. Continue a few short, tree-lined blocks to the end of W. Chestnut. After a RR crossing, enter a park-like area, where you will see the brick DEPARTMENT OF VETERAN'S AFFAIRS MEDICAL CENTER sign directly in front of you.
16.4	**Turn left** onto Fort Walla Walla Recreation Trail, a paved bike and footpath.
17.4	Return to Fort Walla Walla Park and end of ride.

Other Activities In and Around the Route Area

Fort Walla Walla, on the site of an 1858 military reservation, is a feast for kids and history buffs. The complex includes an RV park with hook-ups and tent sites (accessed off Dalles Military Road, phone 509-527-3770), a day use area with picnic facilities and playground equipment, and the museum (both accessed off Myra Road). The museum features a reconstructed pioneer village with cabins, blacksmith shop, jailhouse, train depot, carriage barn and more, displaying many antique items used by early settlers. Five large exhibit halls display hundreds of artifacts including early agricultural implements and modes of transportation. One building shows a full-sized replica of a 33-mule team hooked to an authentic 1919 combine. Hours April through October are Tuesday through Sunday, 10am to 5pm. Call 509-525-7703 for more information.

Seven miles west of Walla Walla (off Highway 12) is another site of historic importance, the Whitman Mission. Built in 1836 by Marcus and Narcissa Whitman, the mission was a place of ministry for the Cayuse Indians (before the misunderstanding that led to the Whitmans' demise) and a supply post for pioneers on the Oregon Trail. Easy trails around the site lead to a panoramic viewpoint.

Downtown Walla Walla is a pleasant and bustling place. A central business and retail core, it has been renovated through a Main Street project with antique streetlamps, benches, and building facades to highlight its historic beauty. Historic buildings near the downtown corridor include the Liberty Theater on Main between First and Colville, built in 1917. Today, its facade is dressed with eagles, stained glass, and terra cotta, and it is part of a department store. Another is the Baker-Boyer Building on the corner of Main and Second. Construction on this building began in the 1800's and was completed in 1910. At seven stories, it was the town's first "skyscraper."

Walla Walla also contains a number of historic homes. For more information about local history and maps, contact the Chamber of Commerce at 509-525-0850. And, if you're more impressed by natural than human history, ask the Chamber for the Blue Mountain Audubon Society's *A Walking Guide to the Big Trees of Walla Walla.*

Finally, if you've heard of Walla Walla, you've heard of Walla Walla Sweets. This world-renowned globe of an onion is so sweet, you can eat it like an apple. Celebrate this gustatory phenomenon at the Walla Walla Sweet Onion Festival weekend in July, or just pick up a bag to share with your friends (June through August). Walla Walla's biggest festival is the Hot Air Balloon Stampede in May. If you plan to visit the community during this festival, make your lodging reservations far in advance.

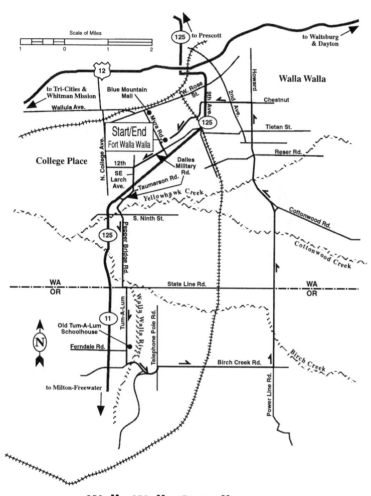

Walla Walla Stateline Loop

● Easy — 17.4 miles

🚲 **14** 🚲

Helix Wheat Country

■ Intermediate — 25.3 miles

Rolling hills.

Highlights
Challenging uphills and exhilarating downhills. The tiny community of Helix (pop. 150).

General Description
Some of eastern Oregon's best cycling is showcased on this "out-in-the-middle-of-nowhere" loop, inspired by the former Helix "Heart ♥ of the Country Biathlon": significant hills on well-paved, two-lane farm roads. The beauty of the landscape and the warmth of the townspeople make it worth the drive. Avoid windy days, which turn this pleasant country ride into an all-out physical challenge.

Start
Reach Helix easily from nearby Pendleton (OR), Umatilla (OR), or Walla Walla (WA). From Pendleton, take Highway 11 or Wildhorse Road northeast to Havana, then take the Havana-Helix Highway north. From Walla Walla, take Highway 125 south, which turns into Highway 11 at the Oregon border. Continue south on Highway 11 until you reach Athena, then follow the signs to Helix. From Umatilla, take Highway 730 east just past Hat Rock State Park to the junction of Highway 37. Proceed southeast on 37 to Holdman, where you will turn left on the Holdman-Helix Highway.

�**OR**� MILEAGE LOG

0.0	Begin at Helix Park, on the west end of town, just north of the Holdman-Helix Highway (Columbia St. as it goes through town). Start from the gravel parking lot between the park and the grain elevators, and **proceed right** (west) on the Helix-Holdman Highway away from town.
0.25	Left intersection with gravel Harper Rd.; pass the grain elevators that are Helix's visual signature. Begin first of the rolling hills. Road is well-

	paved, shoulderless two-lane highway here and throughout the ride. **Continue straight.**
2.8	Left intersection; sign reads Myrick -3. **Continue straight.** Begin 3/4 mile series of **S**-curves.
3.35	Right intersection with Muller Rd. **Continue straight.**
5.5	Intersection with McRae Rd. **Continue straight.**
5.7	Short, steep hill.
6.5	Come to the small farming settlement of Kings Corner; **turn right** on Kings Corner Road. Here's where the rolling hills really start!
8.4	Just after milepost 5, at the bottom of a steep descent, the road forks. **Take the left fork**, following the sign to So. Juniper Canyon Rd. and Helix. Keep an eye out for farm equipment and livestock on and near the roadway throughout the ride.
11.5	Follow as the road makes a **sharp bend to the right**. Gravel South Juniper Road forks off to the left. Begin a steady, winding mile-long climb. (Ya gotta go uphill to get the downhill later!)
13.2	At a **T**-intersection, **take main road to the right** (Juniper Rd.), following the signs to Vansycle and Helix. North Juniper Canyon Rd. goes off to the left. Enjoy the only stretch of straight, flat roadway on the route.
13.8	Left intersection with Stockman Rd. **Continue straight.**
14.4	**S**-curves.
16.3	Begin a long, winding descent that gradually becomes steeper. This exhilarating Juniper Canyon descent lasts over a mile and is the highlight of the ride.
17.5	**Sharp right turn** onto Vansycle Rd. (still descending). Sign reads HELIX – 7.
18.6	Butler Grade/Umapine gravel road intersects on the left.
19.6	South Juniper Rd. intersects on the right, followed almost immediately by a left intersection with Stanton Rd. **Continue straight.**
20.7	Kupers Rd. (gravel) intersects to left. **Continue straight.**
21.75	Long, gentle descent begins.
24.5	Duroc Rd. intersects on the left at an acute angle. Helix comes into view. Roll into town on Harrison Ave. Surface becomes bumpy, patched concrete.
25.3	**Turn right** onto Concord. The city park where you began is one short block in front of you.

Other Activities In and Around the Route Area

This route owes a debt to the wonderful citizens of Helix and the organizers of the former biathlon held there intermittently in the late '80's and early '90's. As Helix modestly (and accurately) described their excellent competition in its 1991 brochure, "The Heart ❤ of the Country Biathlon and the ceremonies in the park which follow are Americana at its best." The biathlon course was ridden clockwise and counterclockwise in alternate years. This ride goes clockwise to take advantage of more right-hand turns and to maximize the rush of descending the Vansycle Canyon hill.

Helix is a warm and unpretentious community. Your most likely greeting committee will be a dog or two—they seem to roam the streets in pairs, wagging their tails in hope of a pat. After my first Helix Biathlon, I was befriended by a one-eyed mongrel who walked in like he owned the place as I nursed a root beer in the local tavern.

Tiny downtown Helix's commercial services mostly straddle Concord (just a block east of the park), and include Helix Lockers, a combination grocery-deli-community gathering place and the Helix Hardware Co., across the street from one another on the corner of Concord and Solar. Around the corner from the grocery entrance, on Solar, is the entrance to Jo's Locker Room, a tavern connected with the store. At the east end of Concord, the attractive edifice of Griswold High School (home of the Grizzlies) rises majestically.

What Helix lacks in amenities can be found in spades in Pendleton, just a few miles south. Pendleton knows all about hosting tourists, due to its world-famous Pendleton Round-up rodeo held each September. Contact its Chamber of Commerce at 1-800-547-8911 or 541-276-7411.

If you're heading north, take a moment to peek at Hat Rock, a volcanic formation that looks...well, just like a hat. It is the central feature of Hat Rock State Park, which also offers camping, picnicking and water access.

The park is located on the Columbia River just off Highway 730 east of Umatilla and Hermiston, right before the Highway 37 cutoff to Helix.

Also be sure to drive through Wallula Gap by taking Highway 730 from Umatilla/Hat Rock east and then north toward Pasco and Walla Walla, Washington. The gap is the carved-out confluence of the Columbia and Walla Walla rivers, just downriver from the great confluence of the Columbia and Snake rivers. This section of the Columbia, behind McNary Dam, is known as Lake Wallula.

Aptly named Hat Rock

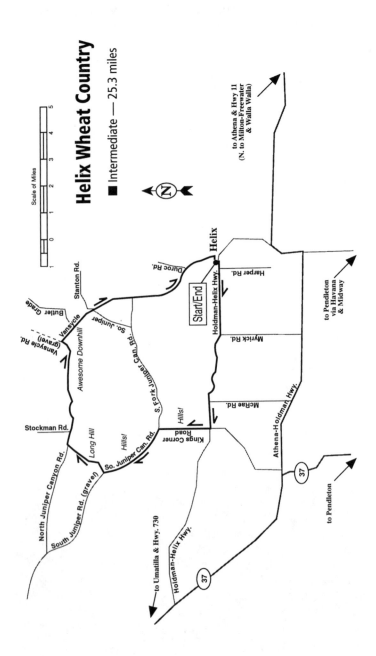

Helix Wheat Country

■ Intermediate — 25.3 miles

Scale of Miles

᪐ **13** ᪐
Heppner Rollers

■ Intermediate — 37.3 miles
Rolling hills.

Highlights
Communities of Heppner and Lexington, rolling prairie.

Route Description
High quality pavement takes you over undulating hills, through rolling prairie grass alternating with cultivated fields. "Wide open spaces!" Many unsigned, mostly gravel, farm roads intersect throughout the route; for the most part, only those roads bearing names and providing useful navigating information are given.

Start
Begin at the Morrow County Fairgrounds on Fairview Way. Find it by locating the elegant old Morrow County Court House, then heading north (left as you face the Court House) on Court until it bends uphill and to the right to become Fairview. The Fairgrounds are on the left.

0❚ MILEAGE LOG

0.0	Leave the parking lot of the Fairgrounds and turn left onto Hwy. 74, which is also Fairview Way. Exercise caution, as this two-lane, well-surfaced, shoulderless road is a highway. As you head east, you are leaving the town of Heppner behind; speed limit increases to 55 mph.
0.9	Cross Hinton Creek. Road is flat and fast.
3.1	**Turn left** on Sand Hollow Rd. Begin ascending into Sand Hollow Canyon. Road surface quality deteriorates a bit; shoulders can be debris-strewn. Scenery consists of rolling prairie grass alternating with wheat fields.
5.3	Gravel road to Lexington intersects on the left. **Continue straight** ahead and uphill, then around a curve and downhill.
5.7	Gravel road forks off to the right; **curve left** and continue on the main, paved road, enjoying a nice downhill.

6.15 | A road forks off to the right and uphill. **Continue straight**, ignoring the fork. You are out in "the rollers" now—plenty of hills, but none particularly difficult or long.

13.5 | Paved road intersects on the right, then curves north to briefly parallel the road you are on; **continue straight** on Sand Hollow Rd., the same road you have been on.

15.0 | T-intersection. **Turn left** on Myers Rd., following the sign toward Sand Hollow and Lexington, rather than right, toward Butter Creek and Pine City.

15.6 | Continuation of Sand Hollow Rd. intersects on the right. **Continue straight** ahead toward Lexington. At the top of the next rise, the road rolls straight out in front of you like an undulating ribbon, swerving neither left nor right. You are surrounded by nothing but fields as far as the eye can see.

18.1 | Follow the road as it makes a 90° bend to the left. Kilkenny Rd., to Hwy. 207, forks off to the right at the bend. **Bend left** with the road, toward East Baseline Rd. and Lexington.

18.6 | 90° bend to the right.

20.3 | Road bends to the left, then right, and begins a gradual slope downhill toward Hwy. 207.

20.8 | Stop-sign intersection with Hwy. 207. Hermiston to the right; **turn left** toward Lexington, being mindful of highway traffic. Visibility limited to the right.

24.55 | Hwy. 207 makes a **90° bend left** as Juniper Canyon Rd. (gravel) intersects on the right. Bend left, continuing to follow the highway.

26.4 | Road to the airport intersects on the right. A long and satisfying descent takes you into Lexington, population 280.

27.0 | Stop-sign intersection with Hwy. 74. Ione and Arlington to the right; **turn left** toward Heppner. You are now on Hwy. 74/207 as you proceed through Lexington, which offers basic services such as a convenience store.

34.1 | Enter the outskirts of Heppner.

35.65 | ENTERING HEPPNER sign. You are on the main thoroughfare of Linden Ave.

36.3 | Historical Marker and park on your right. Marker tells the story of the Heppner Flood of 1903. Picnic area and creek adjacent. This park displays a nice orientation map of the streets of Heppner, and lists another bike route and a walking route.

36.4	Cross Willow Creek.
36.7	**Turn left** on May, following sign toward Hwy. 74/Ukiah. The stately Court House looms in front of you.
36.8	Cross Willow Creek again.
36.9	**Turn left** on N. Court in front of the Court House. Follow Court uphill then as it curves sharply to the right to become Fairview.
37.2	Football stadium on the left.
37.3	**Turn left** into the Morrow County Fairgrounds.

Other Activities In and Around the Route Area

Heppner, an isolated community of some 1450 people, is a fantastic cycling town. It is also the seat of Morrow County and home to the Morrow County Museum. But it is neither the amenities (although they are adequate) nor the tourist attractions that make Heppner a great place to ride—it is the wide-open, gently rolling terrain and the dry, sunny climate. In addition to the route given above, other good routes for cyclists can be found with just a bit of effort. For starters, note the ride shown on the park diorama (at mile 36.3 in the ride above).

The friendly, unjaded, helpful people of the community are another factor that makes Heppner fun. My initial history lesson was provided, unsolicited, by two young boys who told me the building I was admiring—the Morrow County Court House—was built in 1902. It's easy to see why this magnificent blue stone building is the most photographed court house in Oregon. The folks at the Heppner Chamber of Commerce were great, too. Among the most helpful in the state, they ensured me that Heppner would welcome cyclists and provided me with a wealth of information about every conceivable place to stay and to visit in Morrow County. Contact the Chamber at P.O. Box 1232, Heppner, OR, 97836 (541-676-5536).

History buffs should stop at the Morrow County Museum, a collection of regional artifacts and mementos dating back to the mid-1800's. Located on N. Main, hours are 1pm to 5pm Saturday through Wednesday (closed Thursday and Friday). Closed in the month of January. The museum is adjacent to an old one-room school house and the Heppner City Park.

Just north of Heppner, outside the community of Ione, is the Wells Springs pioneer campsite, where you can view the most dramatic Oregon Trail wagon ruts. Take Highway 207 to Ione, then east on Ella Road to the Wells Springs turnoff.

A final plus is accessibility: Heppner is an easy drive from many of the more toured areas of northeastern Oregon—just an hour from Pendleton. The Heppner ride is in close proximity to several other rides in this guide: Helix Wheat Country, Ghost Town Gulch, Fossil Follies, and Ukiah to Hot Springs.

Elegant Morrow County Court House

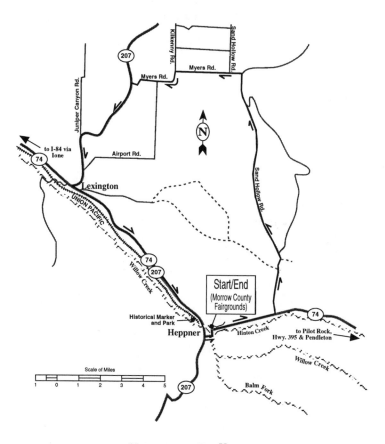

Heppner Rollers

■ Intermediate — 37.3 miles

ᘓᕰ **16** ᘓᕰ
Ukiah to Hot Springs

■ Intermediate — 35.4 miles
Some elevation gain.

Highlights
Town of Ukiah, Lehman Hot Springs, Umatilla National Forest scenery.

Route Description
This out-and-back route travels a beautiful forested road from the friendly community of Ukiah. Head out at an overall but very slight incline along the route of Camas Creek past two United States Forest Service campgrounds to the privately-owned Lehman Hot Springs Resort. Return via the same route, enjoying a net downhill on the return.

As this is a point-to-point ride, those wishing to stay at Lehman Hot Springs could do the route in reverse, making Ukiah the halfway point. Bear Wallow and Lane Creek campgrounds along the route are also alternative start and end points.

Start
Begin in the town of Ukiah, just east of Highway 395 on Highway 244. The 395/244 junction is eighty miles north of John Day and fifty miles south of Pendleton. The ride begins at the northwest corner of the city park on Main/Highway 244 at the information sign describing the Blue Mountain Scenic Byway and the Elkhorn Scenic Byway (see *Other Activities*). Day parking is available around the park.

OH MILEAGE LOG

0.0   From the park, **turn right** (east) on Main/Hwy. 244. Pass the "Antlers Inn" on your left. You can't miss it! It's the only place in town advertising "drop-in showers"—and for a mere $2.00. Leave town on this two-lane, well-paved highway to join and follow Camas Creek.

1.0   Dirt road forks off to the left and uphill. Continue along the main road, with Camas Creek at your right and scenery ranging from meadows to

	granite outcroppings on your left. The road climbs steadily but almost imperceptibly.
5.2	Cable Creek Rd. intersects, then crosses Camas Creek immediately to your right. Continue on Hwy. 244.
9.0	Climb becomes a bit steeper, but still very tolerable.
10.15	UMATILLA NATIONAL FOREST sign on the right, immediately followed by Lane Creek Campground on the left. This no-fee campground, managed by the Umatilla National Forest, provides eight campsites, picnic tables, fire rings, and handicapped-accessible toilets.
10.3	Cross Lane Creek.
11.0	Bear Wallow Campground and Interpretive Trail on the left. This is also a no-fee USFS campground with eight large (over 45 feet in length) campsites. The unique 3/4-mile interpretive trail highlights the life and the environment of the steelhead salmon. Meandering next to Bear Wallow Creek, the barrier-free trail is suitable for all ages.
11.05	Cross Bear Wallow Creek.
12.3	Begin a series of **S**-curves.
14.0	Intersection with gravel USFS Road 54. Cable Creek is 10 miles to the right, Pilot Rock 35 miles to the left.
16.4	**Turn right** toward Lehman Hot Springs.
16.5	Cross over Camas Creek. Patched asphalt road is quite rough.
17.1	*CAUTION!* Cattle-catcher in roadway. Uphill to Lehman Hot Springs.
17.6	*CAUTION!* Pavement ends.
17.75	Lehman Hot Springs; turnaround point. This privately-operated resort features a 9000 square foot natural hot mineral pool, cabin and teepee rentals, RV and tent spaces. Use of the pool is $5.00. Phone 1-800-501-0232 or 541-427-3015 for current rates and information.
18.4	*CAUTION!* Cattle-catcher. Be especially attentive as you travel the exhilarating downhill in this direction. There is no warning sign for the cattle catcher; watch for the yellow poles at either side of the road.
19.0	Cross Camas Creek. Bear left as you prepare to turn back onto Hwy. 244.
19.1	Stop sign. **Turn left** on Hwy. 244 back toward Ukiah.
21.45	USFS Road 54 junction.
24.4	Cross Bear Wallow Creek.
24.45	Bear Wallow Campground and Interpretive Trail on the right.
25.15	Cross Lane Creek.

25.2	Lane Creek Campground entrance on the right.
25.25	LEAVING UMATILLA NATIONAL FOREST sign.
26.0	The ride flattens out and continues fairly flat to Ukiah.
30.2	Cable Creek Road intersects on the left.
34.9	ENTERING UKIAH, POPULATION 250.
35.4	End of ride. City park on your left.

Other Activities In and Around the Route Area

The Ukiah area was originally called Camas Prairie. The town was named "Ukiah" by a settler who missed his native Ukiah, California. The community has a basic infrastructure including lodgings, a trailer park, restaurants, and grocery stores. The area also has fine campgrounds. In addition to Lane Creek and Bear Wallow, Frazier Campground, also operated by the Forest Service, is just a few miles past the Lehman Hot Springs junction on Highway 244. Frazier features 18 campsites and picnic facilities including a group shelter. Purchase a plant identification book from the ranger station in Ukiah and enjoy over 200 species, including wildflowers such as yellow bell, grass widow, and blue violets.

Fifteen miles south of Frazier Campground on gravel USFS Road 5226 is the Tower Mountain Lookout, a forest-fire detection station built in 1929. Ask permission to climb the 106 steps up the 100-foot tower for a great view. Up to four at a time are allowed when the lookout ranger is not too busy.

The North Fork John Day Ranger District office at the west end of Ukiah (0.2 mile west of the city park where the ride begins and ends) is a good source for up-to-date information on camping and other activities in the area. Thanks to Recreation Manager Karen Kendall for her friendly and competent assistance. Contact them at 541-427-3231 or P.O. Box 158, Ukiah, Oregon 97880.

Oregon is full of natural beauty and opportunities for scenic drives. Two such drives are the U.S. Forest Service's Blue Mountain National Scenic Byway and Elkhorn Drive National Scenic Byway. Both are described at the information board from which the bike ride begins. The Blue Mountain Byway takes about five hours. It stretches from the Interstate 84/Highway 74 junction southeast for 130 miles, passing through Ukiah. Terrain ranges from grassland to pine forest to meadows to ancient lava flows. It passes through the town of Heppner (see *Heppner Rollers*), the ghost town of Hardman, and an Oregon Trail junction at Cecil. The Elkhorn Byway is a 106-mile loop out of Baker City (see the next ride), passing through Sumpter, Granite, and the Anthony Lakes Recreation Area. Both scenic drive routes are paved. For information on the Blue Mountain Scenic Byway, contact the Umatilla National Forest office at 541-276-3881; for the Elkhorn Scenic Byway, contact the Wallowa-Whitman National Forest at 541-523-6391.

The Antlers Inn in Ukiah

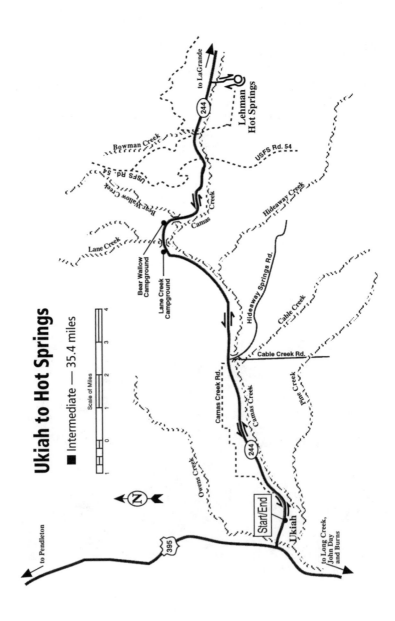

ᕉᕽ **17** ᕉᕽ
Baker City Loop and Mini-Loop

■ Intermediate Loop — 29.7 miles
● Easy Mini-Loop — 12.5 miles

Flat, fast and scenic. The easy loop is especially
suitable for families with school-age children.

Highlights

Idyllic farm scenery on both routes. Wingville township on
the easy route and the village of Haines on the intermediate
route. Be sure to see *Other Activities*, below.

General Description

Flat, fast rides through the wide-open ranch lands of Baker
Valley. Children will enjoy the animals and the farm scenery.
Roads used are moderately well-surfaced, though often
shoulderless, and traffic is light.

Intermediate Loop Start

Begin in front of the Oregon Trail Regional Museum at
Campbell and Grove streets in central Baker City (not to be
confused with the National Historic Oregon Trail Interpretive
Center at Flagstaff Hill just outside of town, which is a must-see,
but not a particularly good cycling destination). The route starts
on Grove Street, between the Museum and Geiser Pollman Park.

OH MILEAGE LOG

0.0	**Turn left** on Campbell St. from Grove St. (*CAUTION:* Campbell St. is a 4-lane thoroughfare, and can be busy); Geiser Pollman Park is now on your left.
0.1	Cross the Powder River.
0.2	**Stay left (straight ahead) at the stop light** intersection with Main St., rather than peeling off to the right. Still on Campbell St., you proceed through a section of stately old residences. The road narrows to two lanes, but remains well-surfaced and wide enough to accommodate cyclists.
0.8	**Turn right** when you reach the stoplight on 10th Street and proceed north through a mixed residential and commercial area.

1.8	Flashing yellow light; Hughes Ln. intersects on the right, becoming Pocahontas Rd. to the left. 10th St. has become Hwy. 30; **proceed straight**, utilizing the shoulder of this two-lane highway that roughly parallels the interstate in the distance to your right (east). You are leaving town behind, and entering long-established farmland; many of the tracts are so old as to display antiquated tractors and other implements.
5.4	Signs indicate a left turn for Wingville Rd./Pine Creek. To the right, at an angle to the northeast, is a gravel road.
6.8	Right intersection with Chandler Ln. Road is well-surfaced and flat.
10.7	Cross Willow Creek.
10.9	Enter the village of Haines. Rodeo grounds on your right. Make sure your water bottles are full before leaving Haines, especially in the warm months.
11.3	**Turn left** on Fourth St., following the sign toward Anthony Lakes ski resort. (Just beyond this turn, the award-winning Haines Steak House is on your right, at the corner of Third Street.) RR Crossing. Rough roadway.
13.0	**Y**-intersection, **take the left fork**, following the sign toward ROCK CREEK — 4, WINGVILLE — 7. Road conditions are still rough.
13.3	Another **Y**. Main road forks to the right. **Take the left fork** again, following the sign toward WINGVILLE and BAKER CITY. You are now paralleling your outbound route.
14.2	Cross Willow Creek.
16.9	Intersection with Hunt Mountain Rd. Slight incline; surroundings become more forested.
18.3	Wingville Rd. intersection on the left: WINGVILLE — 3.
19.8	**Road curves to the left**, sign says BAKER CITY — 7. A dirt road to the right would have taken you to Marble Creek and other outdoor recreational areas.
21.3	90° curve to the right.
21.45	Cross Salmon Creek.
22.05	90° curve to the left.
23.1	Another road intersects on the left, toward Wingville.
23.8	Curve to the right, followed by a curve to the left.
24.0	**Y**-intersection, **take the left fork**.

26.7	RR Crossing; enter the truck-stop end of town. You are entering town on Pocahontas Rd.
27.3	Cross the blinking red light intersection with 10th St./Hwy. 30; the road becomes Hughes Ln. as you **proceed forward.**
28.0	Cross Powder River.
28.5	**Turn right** on N. Cedar St. You are now on an official bike route, heading toward the Baker City downtown business district, through a residential area.
29.5	Cedar St. intersects with Campbell St. The newer business district (chain hotels, fast food, grocery store) is to your left; the older, historic downtown is to your right. **Turn right** on Campbell St.
29.7	Ride ends at Oregon Trail Museum and park. *EXERCISE CAUTION* as you **turn left** from Campbell St. onto Grove St.

Easy Mini-Loop Start

Begin at the blinking-light intersection of Highway 30/10th Street and Pocahontas Road/Hughes Lane at the northwest corner of town. Parking is available at the various truck stop facilities just west of the intersection on Pocahontas or at the State of Oregon Department of Forestry/Department of Fish & Wildlife just east on Hughes Lane.

OM Mileage Log

0.0	Proceed west on Pocahontas Rd., a two-lane well-surfaced but shoulderless road surrounded by pasture land. Elkhorn Ridge rises in front of you.
0.6	RR Crossing.
3.2	Road curves to the right. MARBLE CREEK PICNIC AREA/ WINGVILLE – 3 sign. Ignore the road going off to the left, and **curve right**, followed almost immediately by a **90° bend left**.
4.15	**Turn right**, following sign for WINGVILLE – 3. This road is more roughly surfaced, but still paved. Bucolic scenery features livestock, silos, and tidy farmhouses.
6.75	Stop sign. Pine Creek is to your left; Haines is 6 miles straight ahead; Baker is 7 miles to your right. **Turn right.** Historic Marker at this intersection describes the history of the settlement at Wingville, established in 1862.
8.05	Cross Salmon Creek.

8.5	RR Crossing.
8.8	**T**-intersection with Hwy. 30; **turn right.** Sign indicates Haines is 6 miles to the left (north) and Baker 6 miles to the right (south). Road is well-paved and with shoulders.
12.5	Flashing yellow light; intersection of Hwy. 30 with Pocahontas Rd./Hughes Ln.; end of ride.

Other Activities In and Around the Route Area

The Baker City area is rich with Oregon Trail and general 19th-century history. The Bureau of Land Management's National Historic Oregon Trail Interpretive Center is one of the finest facilities of its kind. Located just outside of town on Highway 86, east of Interstate 84, the center is open year-round (9:00am to 6:00pm May through September, 9:00am to 4:00pm October through April), and admission is free. View both permanent and changing displays, and walk some or all of the 4.2 miles of interpretive trail system, which includes an up-close look at actual Oregon Trail ruts. Phone the center at 541-523-1843 or the Baker County Visitor & Convention Bureau at 1-800-523-1235.

Historic downtown Baker is worth a stroll. Main Street is an eclectic mix of antique shops, souvenir stores, and eateries. Baker is home to 64 historic buildings; a tour map is available from the Visitor & Convention Bureau.

A unique feature of this area is its plethora of genuine gold-rush ghost towns. Pick up a map or guide in town, then visit several within an easy drive from Baker. See Ukiah to Hot Springs, Ride #16, for information on the Elkhorn Drive National Scenic Byway or simply take Main Street south and out of town until it turns into Highway 7 and follow your instincts and occasional signs. Sites include Auburn, Bourne, Whitney, Granite, McEwen, and Sumpter (the latter is still home to a small population, as well as several restaurants and a gas station). If you are in the area on a weekend or holiday between Memorial Day and September, stop off for a narrow-gauge train ride between Sumpter and McEwen. Call 541-894-2268 for departure times.

By the time you have finished either or both of the bike routes, you will understand why the Baker Valley is home to the Haines Steak House. Beef and dairy cattle of many kinds are pastured in this area, and the locals appreciate a good steak.

Voted "Best Steak House in Oregon" by *Oregon* magazine, the Haines Steak House is about 10 miles north of Baker on Highway 30. Open for dinner daily except Tuesdays, 541-856-3639.

Oregon Trail artifacts are abundant in Baker City

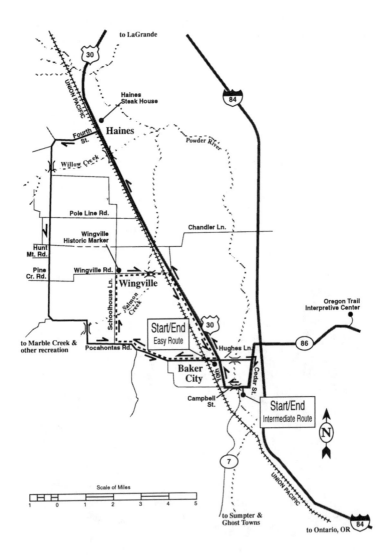

Baker City Loop and Mini-Loop

■ Intermediate Loop — 29.7 miles (——)
● Easy Mini-Loop — 12.5 miles (-----)

᚛ᚉ **18** ᚉ᚛
Wallowa Lake Scenic

■ Intermediate — 26.6 miles

Gentle incline and decline.

Highlights

Wallowa Lake and resort area, Chief Joseph monument, picturesque towns of Enterprise and Joseph.

General Description

Beginning in Enterprise, the route heads south at a very slight but steady incline through farmland at the foothills of the breathtaking Wallowa Mountains, through the historic hamlet of Joseph (named for one of the Chiefs Joseph of the Nez Perce), and along the east shore of Wallowa Lake (the ride includes over eight miles of pristine lakeside cycling). The turnaround is at the south end of the lake, where restaurants and resort activities are available, including the Wallowa Lake Tramway, said to be the world's steepest (open mid-May through September). Retrace the lakeside route to Joseph, and return by a different route to Enterprise, descending all the way. Surfaces are paved but somewhat pock-marked throughout (due to typical precipitation and temperature changes at altitude), with very little shoulder. Caution should be exercised with respect to automobile traffic during peak tourist season.

Start

Reach Enterprise via Oregon State Route 82, also known as the Hells Canyon Scenic Byway, out of LaGrande. Enterprise is about 65 miles from LaGrande and Interstate 84. Begin the ride at the extreme south end of First Street, which is also Highway 3 as it passes through town. South of W. Greenwood Street is a small dead-end "stub" of First Street with numerous parking spots. Note that the Chamber of Commerce, a valuable source of maps and information, is located in the mini-mall across the street.

[0⅄] MILEAGE LOG

0.0	**Turn right** (east) on W. Greenwood St. Proceed one block.
0.1	**Turn right** at the first stop sign, S. River St. Note the historic Court House on the northeast corner to your left and in front of you.
0.2	Cross over Prairie Creek.
0.3	Approaching a **Y** in the road, **take the right fork**, which is essentially straight ahead and says HURRICANE CREEK, as opposed to the left-hand fork, which is Highway 82 to Joseph. The road continues through a mixed-use area of residential and light industrial. The Wallowa Mountains loom in front of you and to your right.
0.7	Cross the Wallowa River.
1.1	Intersection of Farmer's Ln. (to the right) and Green Valley Rd. (to the left), **continue forward**. The magnificent draw you see at about "two o'clock" in the mountain range ahead of you is the canyon formed by Hurricane Creek between Sawtooth Mountain and Chief Joseph Mountain.
1.9	Cross Hurricane Creek.
2.1	Intersection with Eggleson Ln.. At this point, you leave the town of Enterprise behind as you continue south. Hurricane Creek Rd. becomes 2-lane, lightly traveled, shoulderless highway. Irrigation run-off trenches at either side of the road necessitate caution.
4.2	Road makes a **90° bend to the left**.
4.4	**90° bend to the right**.
4.9	Intersection with Russell Rd.; **continue straight ahead.** Farmhouse and barn architecture is at its most quaint through this section.
5.4	Intersection with Pine Tree Rd. (right side only); **continue straight.**
5.6	**Veer left**; a sign indicates that you are now on Airport Ln.
5.7	Cross over Hurricane Creek again, and proceed through a grove of pine trees before emerging into farmland once again. To your right is the thickly-wooded slope of Chief Joseph Mountain.
6.6	**S-curves.**
7.4	Cross Wallowa River and enter the outskirts of Joseph. On your left is the rodeo arena where Chief Joseph Days is proudly held late each July. At this point, Hurricane Creek Rd./Airport Ln. has become Wallowa Ave., on which you are heading east.
7.8	**Turn right** at the stop sign, onto Main St., which is also Highway 82, as well as Joseph-Wallowa Hwy. 10. Joseph is a cute little town with a

	western motif, home to several galleries and the usual assortment of coffee shops, ice cream stands and eateries. Proceed south on Main St.
8.2	Sign indicates a City Park off to the right.
8.8	**S**-curves. **Follow sign pointing left** to WALLOWA STATE PARK – 6.
8.9	Leaving town, road begins to look more like a highway. Note milepost 1. The slight incline you have been enduring becomes steeper and more noticeable here.
9.35	Historical Marker: Chief Joseph monument on the right.
9.4	Wallowa Lake comes into view, as well as its Historical Marker, also on the right. Top-notch photo opportunity. Proceed for the next several miles along this relatively undeveloped lake shore. Pavement is good, but road is shoulderless. Fortunately, there is a guardrail, as well as several pull-out opportunities.
11.9	Milepost 4. Wallowa Lake is nestled amongst various peaks, including Bonneville Mountain, straight ahead at the south end of the lake, and Mount Howard (destination of the tram, also known as the gondola), ahead and slightly to the left.
13.8	Road veers away from the lake.
13.9	The **road forks** as you enter the south end development. To your right is the State Park and campground, as well as private marina featuring various rental craft. Straight ahead is the general store. To your left is the resort area, including the gondola ride, lodging, restaurants and activities such as horseback riding and go-karts.
14.0	**Turn around** at the general store, or stop and explore the resort area. Return mileage is calculated from this **Y**.
16.1	Milepost 4.
17.1	Milepost 3.
18.55	North end of the lake; Wallowa Lake Historical Marker.
18.6	Chief Joseph Historical Marker, after which you enjoy a more substantial downhill grade.
18.9	Creek crossing.
19.1	ENTERING JOSEPH sign and another creek crossing, followed by the **S**-curve that takes you back into town.
19.7	Sign indicating City Park off to the left.
19.85	Wallowa County Museum on the right. This is the downtown section of Joseph. **Continue north** on this road, which is Main St./Wallowa Lake Hwy. 10/Hwy. 82.

20.4	ENTERPRISE/LAGRANDE sign, indicating that Enterprise is 6 miles away.
20.6	Creek crossing.
23.1	Road curves slightly to the left at the intersection with Crow Creek Rd.; signs point to various locations in both directions. **Bear left**, staying on the main road toward Enterprise.
23.3	Cross over Prairie Creek.
25.3	ENTERING ENTERPRISE sign; begin the winding descent into Enterprise.
25.9	Cross over Prairie Creek again, entering commercial development.
26.2	Road forks. **Take the right fork**, following the ELGIN/LAGRANDE, HIGH- WAY 82 sign, as opposed to the HURRICANE CREEK fork that you took earli- er when leaving town. You are now back on S. River St.
26.4	Cross Prairie Creek one last time.
26.5	**Turn left** on W. Greenwood St. (Court House on your right).
26.6	**Turn left** onto the stub of First St. where the ride ends.

Other Activities In and Around the Route Area

As you drive toward Enterprise on Highway 82, stop for current information at the Visitors Information Center in the hardware store at First and Pine in the community of Wallowa. This may not be the largest or best-equipped information center, but the local color and advice are worth a stop. For a more "official" take on things, don't miss the massive U.S. Forest Service ranger station on your left just before you enter Enterprise. Trail and wilderness information can be obtained by phone from the U.S. Forest Service at 541-426-4978 or the Wallowa-Whitman National Forest at 541-523-6391.

The big attraction in this area, year-round, is the lake itself, nestled next to the Wallowa National Forest/Eagle Cap Wilderness, and the resort facilities at the south end. Do take the stunning 20-minute tram (gondola) ride to the top of Mount Howard (541-432-9115), and consider taking an hour or so to wander around the resort area and perhaps catch a bite. "Peak season," when most attractions are open, runs basically from Memorial Day through Labor Day, with the Alpenfest stretching some establishments to late September. But limited services remain available at the south shore of the lake year-round.

If your schedule permits dinner at the lake, try Vali's, a local institution for nearly 20 years. The proprietors are an eastern European couple who—legend has it—fell in love with each other in Los Angeles, then moved to Joseph and fell in love all over again. Reservations are required and the menu is limited but prepared with exquisite care (541-432-5691). Open daily except Mondays during peak season; winters on weekends only.

If you prefer to dine in town, consider Joseph Deli & Catering—so much more than its name implies. During the tourist season, it is a 7-day per week sandwich and Italian deli, but during the off-season, it is an emerging restaurant specializing in a fresh and ever-changing menu of classic French cuisine. Tom, the proprietor, is the menu-maker, head chef and soul of the establishment.

For lighter fare or a sweet treat, try Renee's Gourmet Coffees & Heavenly Treats, just across Main Street in Joseph, or Cloud Nine bakery in Enterprise. More healthfully-inclined appetites will appreciate The Common Good restaurant and store in Enterprise.

Other good-to-know stops in Enterprise include the Book Loft (a nice all-purpose book store with a gallery and coffee bar) and Crosstown Traffic, a bike store with supplies and service capabilities. For more information on the communities, contact the Wallowa County Chamber of Commerce in Enterprise, 541-426-4622 or the Joseph Chamber at 541-432-1015.

Finally, if you're coming all the way to Wallowa Lake, it would be a shame not to visit Hell's Canyon. Ask anyone in Wallowa, Enterprise, or Joseph for their opinion of the best viewing vantage points, and take the time to drive out (some bike it, but many of the roads are not well surfaced for road bikes). For official information, call the Hells Canyon National Recreation Area Headquarters at 541-426-4978.

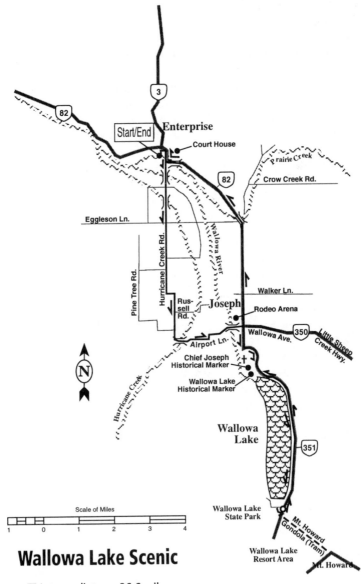

Wallowa Lake Scenic

■ Intermediate — 26.6 miles

ᚨᚦᚨ **19** ᚨᚦᚨ
Ghost Town Gulch

▲ Challenging — 42.7 miles
Hilly.

Highlights
Genuine "ghost town" of Shaniko, hamlet of Antelope, spectacular scenery, and views of Cascade Mountain peaks.

General Description
Rolling hills take you through high desert, timbered canyons and ranch lands, past scenic creeks and through two tiny towns. One significant downhill begins at 13.3 miles, and there is a major, difficult uphill climb out of Antelope from mile 35 to mile 38.

The roadway is well-paved two-lane all the way, with shoulders in places, though not necessarily free from debris. Cyclists are not a frequent sight here, so dress to be seen and ride defensively, especially on the winding canyon roads.

Start
Begin in Shaniko, on Highway 97 north of Bend and south of Biggs. The route is calculated from the corner in front of the Shaniko Hotel and Cafe.

🄾🄼 MILEAGE LOG

0.0	Leave the corner in front of the Shaniko Hotel and head toward Hwy. 97.
0.1	At the stop sign, **turn left** onto Highway 97, following the sign toward Maupin, Madras, and Bend. Exercise caution as you turn onto this highway, crossing traffic. The road is good, two-lane, with shoulders. If the skies are clear, you will see two magnificent snow-capped peaks in front of you in the distance. At "11 o'clock" is 10,405 ft. Mt. Jefferson; at "1 o'clock" is Mt. Hood, Oregon's tallest mountain, at 11,248 ft.
1.7	Bakeoven Rd. intersects on the right, leading toward Maupin. **Continue straight.**

3.3	As you come to the top of a little rise, the triple peaks of the Three Sisters (10,354, 10,053, and 10,004 ft.) come into view to your left.
5.2	SNOW CAP IDENTIFIER pull-out on your right. (Gravel; caution.) Take a moment to stop and become familiar with the several mountain peaks visible from this labeled vantage point. Other peaks visible on a clear day include Mt. Adams, Mt. Rainier, and what remains of Mt. St. Helens. Returning to the highway, the next seven miles are flat or downhill, easy cycling.
12.4	Hwy. 197 junction on the right, toward Maupin and The Dalles. **Curve to the left**, continuing on Hwy. 97 South.
13.3	Rest Area on the right, followed by a 6% downhill grade through Cow Canyon. Enjoy this long, exhilarating downhill into the timbered scenery of the Deschutes recreational area, but watch for asphalt patches on the roadway. A third lane is provided in the middle of the road for uphill traffic, giving motorists additional room to get around you.
20.4	**Turn left**, following the sign toward Antelope, John Day Fossil Beds, and Fossil. This rural road is well-paved, and largely flat for the first few miles, then gently ascending into Antelope.
21.1	ENTERING WASCO COUNTY.
21.3	**Y** in the road. **Take the right fork**, continuing on the main road. The left fork is another road to Maupin.
21.5	Cross Antelope Creek; the road follows to the left of this creek for the next several miles. The timbered surroundings gradually give way to ranch lands and high sagebrush desert as you get closer to Antelope.
29.0	Tub Springs Loop (Lower Tub Springs Rd.) intersects to the right; **continue straight**.
29.6	Cross Indian Creek.
33.1	Tub Springs Loop (Upper Tub Springs Rd.) intersects again on the right; **continue straight**.
33.9	ENTERING ANTELOPE.
34.4	**Y**-intersection with Hwy. 218; **take the left fork** to the stop sign. **Turn left** toward Shaniko, passing through the little community of Antelope on Highway 218/Main Street. Just a few miles from Antelope was the site of the infamous Rajneesh cult compound in the 1980's. The citizens of Antelope seem glad to be rid of this chapter in their local history.
34.6	Antelope Store and Café on the left.

34.9	Leaving Antelope; 55 mph speed limit resumes. Begin a steep, winding, 3-1/4 mile ascent.
35.7	Grade becomes less steep, briefly, before ascending steeply again. Dense sagebrush scenery along this draw is home to a large population of native wildlife, including deer.
38.2	Top of the climb. Vista opens up and Cascade Mountain peaks are in view again. A welcome and gentle descent takes you almost all the way back into Shaniko.
42.1	Black-top road intersects on the right. **Continue straight**, taking a final ascent before Shaniko.
42.5	ENTERING SHANIKO.
42.6	Stop sign. **Turn right** back toward the hotel.
42.7	Ride ends at Shaniko Hotel.

Other Activities In and Around the Route Area

Shaniko, population 25, is a true ghost town, an enigma on a major thoroughfare. Authentic remnants of its boisterous frontier past remain: boardwalks, hitching posts, ramshackle buildings. For many years, the town sat silent, and only recently has begun a tentative restoration.

The centerpiece of the restored community is the historic Shaniko Hotel, (541-489-3441 or 1-800-483-3441). A 17-room bed-and-breakfast facility, the hotel is a charming restoration. The café (open 7:00am to 9:00pm during the spring and summer, and 7:00am to 7:00pm in the winter) offers well-prepared, if standard, fare. Breakfasts are good, the only unusual offering being trout. Dinners cater to the meat-eating palate: steaks, ribs, chops, and the like. The hotel is also the registration point for The Shaniko RV Corral, a park with 10 hook-ups, 50 non-hook-up sites, and basic facilities including showers, laundry, propane, and dump station.

Other services include the Shaniko Wedding Chapel, offering "real old west weddings" (for information, call 541-246-4093), an old-time photo studio, and antique and gift shops. Shaniko remains low-key and not heavily commercialized. Most of the buildings and old west artifacts around town are genuine period pieces.

From Antelope, it is an easy and scenic drive east on Highway 218 to the Clarno Unit of the John Day Fossil Beds National Monument. See the next ride, *Fossil Follies*, for information on this fascinating area.

to Maupin

to Biggs

Bakeoven Rd.

97

197

Snow-Cap
Identifier

Shaniko

Start/End

218

Ward Creek

Indian Creek

Antelope

Rest Area

to Fossil

218

COW CANYON

Upper Tub Springs Rd.

Antelope Creek

Lower Tub Springs Rd.

N

Ghost Town Gulch

▲ Challenging — 42.7 miles

97

to Bend

Scale of Miles

1   0   1   2   3   4   5   6   7   8   9   10

ᨠᩮ **20** ᨠᩮ
Fossil Follies

● Easy — 6.4 miles

Fairly flat out-and-back course.

Highlights

John Day Fossil Beds' Sheep Rock Visitor Center, Blue Basin fossil site trails.

General Description

Short point-to-point ride designed to give a glimpse of the best of far-flung John Day Fossil Beds National Monument. Starts at the Sheep Rock Visitor Center (see *Other Activities*, below) and turns around at the Blue Basin fossil trails to retrace the first half of the ride. A lack of paved alternative roads in this area makes this a simple out-and-back route. Bring a lock and lock your bikes at the Blue Basin trailheads to enjoy a moderate hike at the ride's halfway point.

Start

From Highway 26, between John Day and Prineville, take Highway 19 North. Sheep Rock Visitor Center is on your right just a few miles north of the 19/26 junction. From Fossil (a good place to stay when planning to spend more time exploring the Fossil Beds Monument), take Highway 19 South through Service Creek, Spray, and Kimberly.

Start your trip by taking a stroll through the Visitor Center, where you can get maps to better understand the layout of this area

🆗 MILEAGE LOG

0.0	Begin at the stop-sign exit to the Visitor Center parking lot. **Turn right** to head north on Hwy. 19. Roadway is moderately well-paved with a rough shoulder. The John Day River flows alongside you on the right, and you are headed up a slight incline.
1.5	Goose Rock on your right. Continue at a slight incline through cattle ranch and high sagebrush desert country, flanked by hillocks sporting basalt outcroppings.

2.3	Cross the John Day River.
2.8	Sign for BLUE BASIN TRAILHEAD.
3.2	**Turn right** into the Blue Basin area parking lot, turning off your mileage computer. Lock your bike and take time to explore one or both of the trails (information below). Restart your computer as you leave the parking lot. From the Blue Basin area parking lot, **turn left on Hwy. 19**, paralleling the John Day River on your right. Slight downhill.
4.0	Cross the John Day River.
4.8	Goose Rock on your left.
6.4	**Turn left** into Sheep Rock Visitor Center.

Activities In and Around Route Area

John Day Fossil Beds National Monument is part of the National Park Service, and consists of three units: Sheep Rock (the focus of this ride); Clarno (on Highway 218 between Antelope and Fossil); and Painted Hills (on Highway 26 just west of the 26/207 junction). All can be visited in a day, but the drive between each of the units can take an hour or more.

Touchable display at Sheep Rock Visitor Center

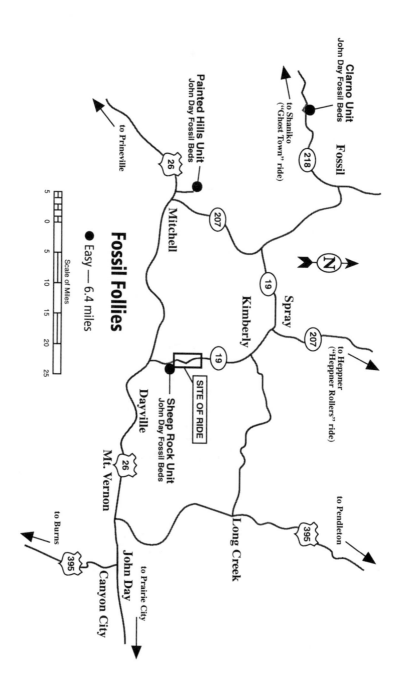

Fossil Follies
● Easy — 6.4 miles

SITE OF RIDE

Sheep Rock Unit
John Day Fossil Beds

Clarno Unit
John Day Fossil Beds

Painted Hills Unit
John Day Fossil Beds

Fossil

Mitchell

Spray

Kimberly

Dayville

Mt. Vernon

Long Creek

John Day

Canyon City

to Shaniko
("Ghost Town" ride)

to Prineville

to Heppner
("Heppner Rollers" ride)

to Pendleton

to Burns

to Prairie City

Scale of Miles

5   0   5   10   15   20   25

۶۶ **21** ۶۶
Vale-on-the-Trail

● Easy — 19.8 miles.
Some hills.

Highlights
Views of rural Malheur County, easy cycling, charming and historic downtown Vale.

General Description
Loop route from the village of Vale (population 1605), site of extensive Oregon Trail history and home to a developing gallery of murals. The first half of the ride is basically uphill, but not arduous, leaving the community and traveling through farmland on the outskirts. The return is downhill and ends by going through tiny, well-kept downtown Vale.

Start
Approach from Highway 20/26 West. If you approach Vale heading east, you must proceed through town on the one-way main street and make a U-turn back into Vale on the westbound route. Immediately upon entering the town westbound, turn into a large gravel parking lot on your right. The parking lot contains a Historical Marker kiosk commemorating Stephen Meeks' Cutoff. Meeks was a member of an Oregon Trail party that passed through the area that is now Vale in the 1840's. Irritated by the slow pace of the group, Meeks convinced 200 families to attempt a shortcut across Oregon. Twenty-four lives were lost before the ill-fated band reconnected with the main party at The Dalles. This site also describes the Blue Bucket gold rush, a phenomenon prompted by members of Meeks' party who, in an attempt to find water, stumbled upon a small amount of gold. The ride begins from this parking lot.

[OM] MILEAGE LOG

0.0	Upon leaving the parking lot, **turn right** on the one way main street (Court St. N., also Hwy. 20/26) and immediately bear left at the **Y**. *EXERCISE CAUTION* as you cross to the left-hand lane, following the sign to Hwy. 20 rather than the right-hand fork to Hwy. 26.
0.3	Vale's Visitor Center/Chamber of Commerce is one block to the right, at 275 Main St.
0.5	A sign indicates that Vale's City Center is to your left; continue straight.
0.85	Take the **right fork** at the **Y**, toward Bully Creek, rather than the left fork toward Juntura/Burns.
1.3	Begin short, steep uphill grade (0.4 miles). The next several miles will be a net uphill.
1.9	Another slight rise. You are now pedaling through the outskirts of Vale.
2.4	Downhill.
2.6	Right-hand intersection with Birch Rd.
2.9	Short, steep descent, followed immediately by a sharp 0.4-mile ascent. At the top of the ascent, the view opens up and Double Mountain is visible to the south.
3.6	Intersection with Cedar Rd. Be aware that the road you are on is a primary road for the local farm traffic, and you are likely to encounter machinery in the road. This is not a heavily touristed area, and the locals are likely to smile and wave you by.
4.65	Intersection with Greenfield Rd.
5.5	Begin a descent. Watch for gravel and debris over this stretch, as the sides of the road are steeply banked.
6.1	Sign for BULLY CREEK JUNCTION.
6.45	Bully Creek Rd. intersects to the right; Bully Creek Reservoir is 4 miles to the right.
6.7	Creek crossing. You are now leaving cultivated land behind and entering a more sparsely populated section of unimproved land.
7.1	Begin a 0.6-mile ascent, at first gradual, then steeper.
7.8	Top of the hill. **Turn left** on Graham Blvd. Heading south, you are once again surrounded by cultivated farmland. Sourdough Mountain and Double Mountain are visible in front of you, with other buttes and hills ringing the valley on all sides. The road gently descends.

8.8	Road makes a right-angle **bend to the left**.
9.1	At the **Y, take the right fork**, continuing on Graham Blvd. (Left fork is Whitney.) Begin a 3/4-mile winding descent into a shaded canyon.
10.4	Left intersection with Country Ln. (gravel), after which the road curves to the right.
11.0	RR Crossing.
11.3	Road curves to left toward Hwy. 20.
11.5	**T**-intersection with Hwy. 20. **Turn left**, back toward Vale.
12.9	Left intersection with Hope Rad. A sign indicates that Bully Creek is to the left. This section of highway is well-maintained and lightly traveled, with a good shoulder, especially in the eastbound direction.
14.6	Right intersection with Russell Rd.
17.1	Cross Bully Creek.
18.3	ENTERING VALE sign. Note the Bates Motel on your right (are they serious?) As Hwy. 20 goes through Vale, it divides into two one-way streets. This right-hand, eastbound street is the main downtown corridor.
18.75	Starlite Cafe on the left, home to such hearty American home cookin' as biscuits and sausage gravy.
18.8	The Caf-A Connection, also on the left, offers a wide variety of deli sandwiches and properly crafted espresso drinks.
19.4	Cross Malheur River, get in left lane.
19.6	**Turn left** in preparation to make the **U**-turn back into Vale westbound. Yield to westbound traffic on Hwy. 20/26 and re-cross the river.
19.8	**Turn right** into the parking lot from which you began.

Other Activities In and Around the Route Area

The community of Vale offers sufficient charm and amenities to merit an overnight stay. While trading heavily on Oregon Trail memorabilia, it also makes an effort to provide a full complement of modern services. This results in such amusing incongruities as "The Oregon Trail Tanning Salon" (One wonders, "Did the pioneers have to worry about this?")

The Oregon Trail did, in fact, pass right through the area that is today Vale. A map painted handily on the side of the Dairy Queen is perhaps a visitor's best source of orientation. For the best in authentic Oregon Trail lore, be sure to go south on Lytle

Boulevard, where your route retraces a section of the trail. Stop at Keeney Pass and see actual wagon-wheel ruts from the passage of the pioneers. Also on this stretch of road is the Henderson gravesite, a reminder of the thousands who met death on the Oregon Trail.

Driving east from Vale on Highway 20/26 toward Ontario, you will see Malheur Butte, remnant of ancient volcanic times, and the Nevada Ditch, a hand-dug irrigation trench dating from 1881 and still in use today. Both are further explained by Historical Marker signs along the route. Within Vale, a short walk will take you on a tour of 16 historic buildings, including the Rinehart Stone House (1872), Vale Hotel (1908), and Opera House (1902). A descriptive brochure and map is available from the Chamber of Commerce at 275 N. Main Street, (541-473-3800). Also enjoy the expanding collection of murals sprinkled throughout town; the Chamber can provide you with the current list.

Note that Malheur County is also the site of Owyhee Lake and the Owyhee Loop ride (#22 in this book). For more information and nearby activities, see the Owyhee listing. These two rides could easily be combined in one weekend.

Oregon Trail mural in Vale

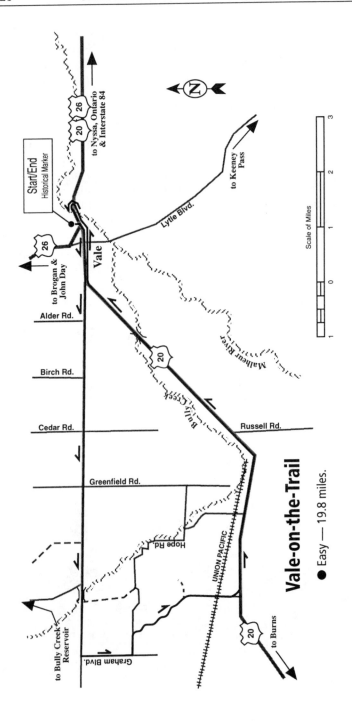

Vale-on-the-Trail

● Easy — 19.8 miles.

🚲 **22** 🚲
Owyhee Loop

■ Intermediate — 32.0 miles
Relatively flat.

Highlights

Two crossings of the Snake River; Oregon Trail Historical Marker commemorating the original Snake River Crossing; town of Nyssa and hamlets of Owyhee Corner and Adrian.

General Description

This relatively flat route rolls through farmland and small villages, looping into Idaho. Moderate to good road surfaces, two easy and scenic Snake River crossings. There are few turns on the route. Most road intersections are listed for verification of route and mileage; turn only if a turn is specified.

Start

To access the ride's start at Owyhee, follow I-84 southeast to Ontario, Oregon, just west of where I-84 crosses into Idaho. At Ontario, look for the exit to Business Route 201. Follow the signs toward Nyssa and Lake Owyhee. In Nyssa, watch for a right-hand turn to continue on 201. Owyhee, also known as Owyhee Corner, is south of Nyssa on 201.

🔲 MILEAGE LOG

0.0	Begin at Owyhee, at the grocery store at the intersection of Owyhee Ave. and Hwy. 201. (Going west on Owyhee Ave. from this junction leads to the lake). **Turn right** out of the grocery-store parking lot and head south toward Adrian on Hwy. 201.
0.7	Right-hand intersection with River Rd., immediately followed by crossing the Owyhee River. As you continue south, Brown Butte, Deer Butte, and Mitchell Butte are visible ahead and to your right.
1.5	Top of incline; vista opens up to the left, affording view of Snake River canyon.
2.2	Intersection; signs indicate KINGMAN COLONY to the left and LAKE OWYHEE STATE PARK — 25 to the right.

2.8	*EXTREME CAUTION:* bad angle railroad track; swerve to take it perpendicular. Follow road as it curves right.
3.3	Mendiola Road intersects at right.
3.8	ENTERING ADRIAN, POPULATION 150. Adrian High School on the left.
4.1	"Adrian Merc" grocery store, followed by cafe and tavern, all on the left.
4.6	**Turn left**, following signs to Parma, Wilder, and Caldwell (Idaho). Note Oregon History marker on your left at the turn.
4.8	Cross Snake River.
5.2	**T**-intersection with Big Bend Road. **Turn left** toward Roswell and Parma.
5.45	*CAUTION:* **sharp bend to the right.** Road surfaces rougher through this section, with asphalt patching in places. Open farmland, largely corn, dominates the scenery.
6.0	Slight incline begins at the intersection of gravel Miller Ave.
6.5	Gravel road intersection at right with Primrose Rd.
7.0	Gravel road intersection at right with Cassia Rd.
7.45	Road makes a **sharp left**, becoming State Line Rd. Continue to follow signs toward Roswell and Parma.
7.5	**Right turn** follows almost immediately (stay on same road).
7.7	**90° bend to the left.**
8.7	Road makes a **right hand-bend** on to Hwy. 18. Rural self-styled antique shop on the left. Asphalt surfaces are somewhat irregular.
10.1	Canal crossing and right-hand intersection with Pebble Ln.
11.35	ROSWELL ROAD and REDUCED SPEED signs indicate your entrance to the community of Roswell.
11.8	Roswell Quick Mart on the right.
12.4	4-way stop; **turn left** (route of Hwy. 18 also turns left here) toward Parma.
13.7	Intersection with Lee Ln.
13.9	Boise River crossing. Road surfaces improve as you approach Parma.
14.6	Enter Parma city limits; road curves to right.
15.05	RR Crossings.
15.15	Intersection of Hwy. 18 and Hwy. 95/20/26. Signs indicate that Payette is to your left and Caldwell to the right. **Turn left.** (Town of Parma lies immediately to the right.) Gradual incline and ample shoul-

	ders for the next 3/4 mile on this well-surfaced highway, which is a part of the Oregon Trail Auto Route.
15.4	NYSSA — 8 MILES sign, followed by cemetery on left.
16.6	Intersection with Klahr Rd. You'll be glad you brought water along on this wide-open stretch, particularly in the sizzling summer months.
17.2	Begin an uphill.
18.0	Top of hill; begin 1/4-mile decline. Gentle rolling hills from here.
18.8	ENTERING PAYETTE COUNTY.
19.7	Intersection with Grandview Rd, just past milepost 52.
21.3	**Turn left** at Anderson Corner, parting company with Hwy. 95 and continuing on Hwy. 20/26 West. Road texture becomes rougher, patchy in places, and road is shoulderless.
22.2	Begin descent toward the Snake River, curving slightly to the right before intersecting Apple Valley Rd. Use caution as you approach the bridge; merging traffic on the right (you have the right-of-way.)
22.8	WELCOME TO OREGON; re-cross Snake River.
23.0	ENTER NYSSA—THUNDEREGG CAPITAL OF THE WORLD—POPULATION 2850. If you can ignore the slight industrial blight ahead on the left, the river is lovely.
23.35	Pass under railroad overpasses and proceed straight ahead on Nyssa's Main St.
23.5	Visitor's Center and Chamber of Commerce off to the left.
23.8	**Turn left** at the Nyssa Elementary, following signs to Hwy. 201 South/Adrian.
24.0	Pass Nyssa Middle School and the Oregon Trail Arena.
24.6	Note old stone house foundation and freestanding masonry chimney off to the right of roadway.
25.1	Main road **curves to left**, becoming Clark Blvd. Continue on this road through a series of right-angle bends left and right over the next few miles. Its name becomes Enterprise Ave.
28.0	Intersection with Grand Ave.
28.9	Historical Marker commemorating the Oregon Trail's Snake River Crossing.
29.0	**Right-hand 90° bend** in road.
29.9	Road makes **left-hand, 90° bend** at Fairview Dr.
32.0	Return to Owyhee corner grocery store.

Other Activities In and Around the Route Area

A major recreational attraction is Lake Owyhee, a 55-mile-long dammed section of the Owyhee River just west of our ride. Resort facilities including cabins, a restaurant, marina with boat launch and rentals, and RV parking are located at the north end of the lake, accessible via Owyhee Avenue off Highway 201, phone 541-339-2444. Much of the lake, which is filled with crappie and bass, is accessible only by boat. The Owyhee River is a site for kayaking and river rafting, and the 417-foot-high Owyhee Dam is known for its unique "glory hole" spillway.

Don't forget your high-clearance four-wheel-drive vehicle for exploring Succor Creek State Recreation Area, 73 miles south of Nyssa. Take Highway 201 (the same route used at the beginning of the bike ride) south past Adrian, then fork right on Succor Creek Road when 201 branches left toward Idaho. Spectacular scenery and rockhounding (see below). Check with the Bureau of Land Management (541-473-3144) for road conditions. Just a short drive farther south is Three Fingers Rock and the fascinating rock formations of Leslie Gulch Canyon. View pinnacles, spires, and towering rock walls along this nearly 10-mile canyon. Wildlife, including bighorn sheep, are often spotted, especially near dawn and dusk. Remember to bring drinking water when visiting these remote and primitive sites.

The gulches and canyons of this area are a rockhounding paradise. Take time to comb the Succor Creek area for Thundereggs, the official Oregon state rock. These egg-shaped geodes are usually russet in color, and filled with opal or chalcedony. Nyssa, the self-proclaimed "Thunderegg Capital of the World," hosts Thunderegg Days, a festival of rocks and gems, for five days beginning the second Wednesday each July. Contact the Nyssa Chamber of Commerce at 541-372-3091 for more information on Thunderegg Days, rockhounding, or lodging.

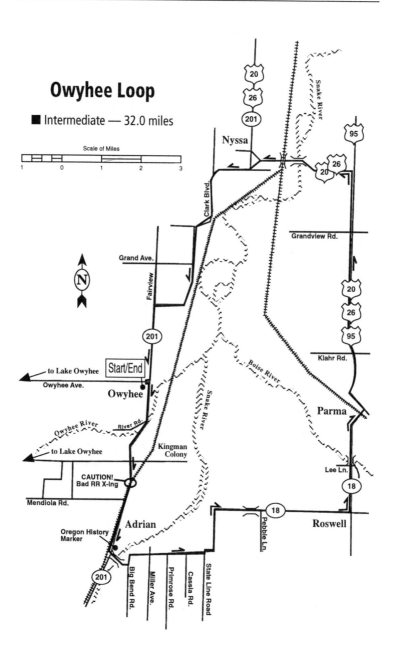

Owyhee Loop

■ Intermediate — 32.0 miles

᚛᚛ **23** ᚛᚛
Harney Valley Big Ol' Flat

▲ Challenging — 72.5 miles
■ Intermediate — 30.4 miles
Fast and flat.

Highlights
Community of Burns, sagebrush desert and ranch land scenery. The longer ride also goes through the tiny outpost of Buchanan.

Route Descriptions
If you like it fast and flat, these are the rides for you. For the long ride, travel east from Burns on Highway 20 to Buchanan, turning south just in time to miss a major hill. From Buchanan, head south toward Crane, turning onto Highway 78 (Steens Highway) to head west and then northwest back to Burns. Well-paved two-lane highway all the way, light traffic, and more visibility than you need make this long loop almost easy. *Bring water*, because there is no relief from the summer's sun here in big ol' flat Harney Valley. All roads used on this route are classified as "Most Suitable" (the highest designation) for bicyclists according to the Oregon Department of Transportation.

The intermediate ride begins the same way, but turns north off Highway 20 to loop through Harney before returning to Burns.

Start
Begin at the Safeway grocery store on Monroe/Highway 20/395 in Burns.

Challenging Ride

OM MILEAGE LOG

0.0	Leave on the east side of the parking lot, **turning left** onto Buena Vista. By using Buena Vista, a quiet residential street, you parallel the main road through Burns and avoid the central downtown corridor. Be

alert, however, as you pass a couple of intersections with no stop signs in any direction.

0.2	Harney County Court House on the left. **Turn right** on W. A St.
0.3	Stop sign a N. Alvord; **continue straight**.
0.35	Stop sign; **turn left** on N. Broadway.
0.55	Historic Museum and Visitor Information Center on your left. Continue to follow this main road (N. Broadway/Hwy. 395/Hwy. 20) north through town.
0.65	City park on the left. Past the park, you begin to leave Burns and the speed limit increases to 45 mph. The road is two-lane, with somewhat rough pavement and shoulders.
1.1	Cross Silvies River; speed limit increases to 55 mph. Burns, as a major junction for interstate truck traffic, offers truck-stop facilities and a weigh station along this corridor; be alert to resulting cross traffic.
1.7	County Rd. 119 intersects on the left.
2.9	**Y**-intersection. **Stay right**, taking Hwy. 20 East toward Vale and Ontario. The left fork goes onto Hwy. 395 North toward John Day. Hwy. 20 is a two-lane road with modest shoulders. Maintenance construction was begun on this road in 1995 and is scheduled to continue on sections between Burns and Buchanan until August 1996. The road will be passable at all times, but slight delays may be experienced.
5.1	Harney County Rd. 116/Red Barn Lane intersects on the right, followed by a slight 0.4 mile incline.
7.2	Right-hand intersection with paved road. As you head out across the Harney Valley, the Stinkingwater Mountains are in view ahead and slightly to the left. Depending upon visibility, you may also see the Crane Mountains ahead and off to the right.
8.3	Left-hand intersection with County Rd. 104. This is the point from which the shorter, intermediate route (see ride description following) will re-enter Hwy. 20 on its return to Burns.
13.5	Intersection with paved Rattlesnake Rd. on the left (toward Harney and Call Meadows) and gravel Lawen-Harney Rd. on the right. A Historical Marker regarding Fort Harney, an American military fort originally about 2-1/2 miles to the north, is on the southeast corner of the intersection. *TURN LEFT FOR THE SHORTER, INTERMEDIATE ROUTE* (see below); for the long route, **continue straight** ahead on Hwy. 20.
17.4	County Rd. 101 (also known as Cow Creek Rd.) intersects on the left.

21.7	Road begins to curve gently to the left. Over the next few miles, you become acutely aware that the road ahead is about to climb—and rather steeply—directly up into the Stinkingwater Mountains.
24.7	Saved! Just before the road ascends, you arrive at the tiny outpost of Buchanan—a store, "museum" of sorts, gift shop and gas station. Take the **acute angle right turn**, following the sign for Crane and avoiding the hill. The roadway continues to be flat and fast, and the blacktop is smooth.
25.3	Cross Little Rock Creek.
28.1	**90° bend in the road to the left**, skirting the base of a low, sage-covered hill. The Stinkingwater Mountains—such an unlovely name for such a majestic sight—rise dramatically in front of you.
30.3	Creek crossing.
30.4	**90° bend to the right**, heading due south again.
42.6	Stop-sign intersection; Crane is to your left. **Turn right**, pass a yield sign and merge onto Hwy. 78 (also known as Steens Highway) headed back toward Burns. This patchy, two-lane, shoulderless road is lightly traveled and flat as can be.
44.3	Road begins to curve to the left to head due west. To your left (south) is Saddle Butte, beyond which lie Malheur Lake and the Malheur National Wildlife Refuge (see *Other Activities*).
45.8	Crystal Crane hot tub spa, RV park and cabins on your right.
46.3	Gravel road intersects on the right, immediately followed by a gravel road intersecting on the left.
49.5	Newton Rd. intersects on the right.
53.5	Road curves gently to the right and passes under power lines, heading northwest toward Burns.
54.7	Lawen Store on your left.
56.5	Sealy Ln. intersects at an angle on your left (heading south); the gravel road intersecting to the right is the road from Lawen to Harney.
58.0	County Rd. 110/Embree Bridge Rd. intersects on the left.
60.2	County Rd. 106A/Hutchenson Rd. intersects on the right.
62.5	County Rd. 111/Oil Well Rd. intersects on the left.
65.4	Intersection to both left and right. County Rd. 112/Faye Ln. goes to the left and back; to the right and back is County Rd. 113/Rye Grass Ln.; to the right and ahead is County Rd. 114/Old Expr. Sta. Rd. **Continue straight** on the main road, Hwy. 78.

68.3	Road curves to the left. Airport Rd. goes off to the right.
69.05	Ditch crossing.
69.5	Another ditch crossing.
70.5	Intersection with Hwy. 205. Frenchglen and Malheur National Wildlife Refuge to the south.
71.4	Cross Silvies River.
71.6	Right intersection with Koa Ave.
71.8	Entering Burns, Population 2915. Exercise caution as you enter town, due to local cross traffic as well as interstate truck traffic.
72.3	Stop-light intersection. John Day/Vale, Hwy. 395/20 to the right; Lakeview/Bend, Hwy. 20/395 straight ahead. **Go straight ahead.**
72.5	Finish at the Safeway parking lot on your right.

Intermediate Ride

Follow the route of the Challenging Ride to the 13.5 mile point.

[OM] MILEAGE LOG

13.5	**Turn left** toward Harney.
15.2	Cross over a ditch.
15.3	Road intersects on the right.
15.55	**Turn left** on Harney County Rd. 104/North Harney Rd.
16.1	Road makes a bend to the left.
16.7	**S**-curve.
17.0	Pass a weathered, old wooden house with a rock chimney on the left, just before a creek crossing.
17.9	Stop-sign **T**-intersection with Harney County Rd. 105/Reed Rd.; **turn left**.
18.4	Road makes a 90° bend to the right.
19.45	Ditch or creek crossing.
20.3	Road curves to the left, then begins a series of **S**-curves toward the highway.
21.75	Sharp bend to the left.
22.1	**T**-intersection back into the highway. **Turn right.**
23.05	Paved road intersects on the left.

25.1	Left intersection with Red Barn Ln.
27.3	Road forks; **take the left fork** toward Burns. *CAUTION: DIFFICULT MERGE* as Hwy. 395 intersects from the right, especially at 27.5.
28.5	County Rd. 119 intersects on the right. You are heading back into Burns.
29.1	Cross Silvies River.
29.6	City Park on the right.
29.75	Intersection with D Street; museum and Visitor Information Center on the right. Continue straight ahead on N. Broadway, using caution as you travel down the main corridor of town.
29.9	Wayside Delicatessen on the right.
30.1	Post Office on the right.
30.2	Stop-light intersection with Highway 78/W. Monroe Street. **Turn right**, following signs toward Lakeview/Bend/Highway 395/20.
30.4	Turn right into the Safeway parking lot to finish the ride.

Other Activities In and Around the Route Area

Burns, along with its nearby sister city of Hines, has a combined population of just over 4000, yet this self-contained community is the ideal (and, for all practical purposes, the *only*) staging point for exploring wide-open Harney County. A vast county, Harney is larger than some entire states. It is part of the Great Basin, with its own elaborate ecosystem ranging from sagebrush steppe to mountains, lakes, marshes and aspen groves. It is best explored slowly, quietly, with binoculars in hand.

Burns itself, a long-established junction for interstate truck traffic, does not generally see itself as a tourist destination. Ten years ago, a bicycle tourist would have been largely unheard of. Today, bike touring is not exactly commonplace, but you will not be treated as though you had just beamed in from a distant galaxy.

While in Burns, try a bite, or at least a latté, from the Wayside Delicatessen Company, one of the more toothsome spots along N. Broadway, where freshly-prepared choices include two different vegetarian sandwiches. For additional information on tourist amenities, contact the Harney County Chamber of Commerce at 541-573-2636. In town, stop by the Visitor

Information Center and Harney County Museum, both located just off Broadway at 18. W. D St.

Three distinct natural areas lie south of the ride route and within an easy drive from Burns: Malheur National Wildlife Refuge, Diamond Craters, and Steens Byway.

The Malheur Wildlife Refuge, a 193,000-acre area centered around Malheur Lake, is a bird-watching paradise. Canadian geese, trumpeter swans, eagles, hawks, blackbirds, bluebirds and more species frequent the area, particularly in the spring and fall. The refuge headquarters is 30 miles south of Burns.

For a geological experience that is so unique it's almost obscure, Diamond Craters is just a bit farther south off Highway 205. This in-situ "museum of basaltic volcanism" offers a look at lava flows, cinder cones, domes, craters, and other volcanic evidence that brings scientists from all over the world. Diamond Craters may not look like much to the untrained eye, but with the help of Bureau of Land Management literature (phone 541-573-5241), anyone with a reliable vehicle, sturdy shoes, and a canteen can become an amateur geologist as they explore this 6-mile-diameter lava pancake.

Steens Mountain National Backcountry Byway is a scenic 66-mile drive offering a sampling of the best of eastern Oregon's "outback." Access the route from Frenchglen, a tiny hamlet with basic services including dining, lodgings, gas, and a store about 60 miles south of Burns on Highway 205. The drive is a rough and rocky one not recommended for motor homes, trailers, or low-clearance vehicles. Its 66-mile course takes you past geological faults and glacially-formed gorges, historic ranches and native flora, and areas roamed by wild horses, antelope, bighorn sheep and elk. The route is usually open July 1-October 31, with parts sometimes open earlier and later. Contact the Burns District of the Bureau of Land Management (see telephone number above) for more information.

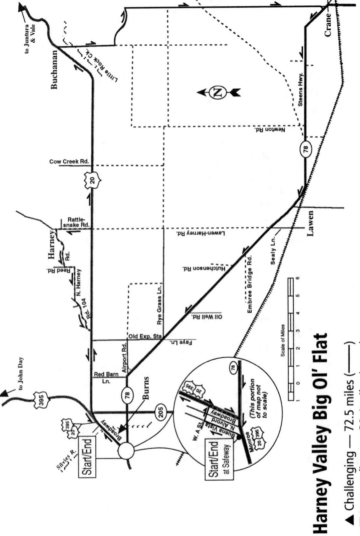

Harney Valley Big Ol' Flat

▲ Challenging — 72.5 miles (———)
■ Intermediate — 30.4 miles (- - - - -)

᧗ **24** ᧗
Silver Lake Forest Loop

■ Intermediate — 41.3 miles

Rolling hills.

Highlights
Beautiful woodland scenery, Thompson Reservoir.

Route Description
Rolling ride on county and Forest Service roads through Fremont National Forest. This outstanding route was conceived by Rick and Marilyn Elston and Don Gay, and is unusual in its combination of scenic beauty and well-paved but lightly travelled roads. In fact, the only flaws in this otherwise perfect ride are the numerous "cattle catcher" gratings along the roads, all of which are indicated in the mileage log. These widely-spaced metal gratings span the road for the purpose of discouraging animals from crossing, but are equally discouraging—and downright dangerous—to cyclists. Be safe by noting their locations and walking your bike across them.

Start
The ride begins at the Fremont National Forest's Silver Lake Ranger Station, just west of the town of Silver Lake off of Highway 31 (look for the tall blue water tower). Inquire at the ranger station as to the best place to park your vehicle. The staff is among the most friendly and helpful I have ever encountered; utilize their knowledge of roads, camping, wildlife and points of interest to enhance your stay in the Silver Lake area.

0⃞5⃞ Mileage Log

0.0	Leave the ranger station and head back toward the main road (Hwy. 31). **Caution: cattle catcher** grating in the road as you leave the parking lot. Table Rock visible ahead and slightly to the right.
0.2	**Caution: another cattle catcher.**
0.3	Stop sign. **Turn right** on Hwy. 31.
0.4	**Turn right**, following signs for East Bay Campground and Hager Mountain Trail. This road is also known as East Bay Rd., or Lake

	County Rd. 4-12. (It is also signed as being Forest Service Rd. 28, although it is not technically a USFS road until it passes the National Forest boundary.) Roadway is smooth, paved two-lane; scenery is sagebrush desert.
2.7	*CAUTION:* cattle catcher.
4.0	At around this point, the desert begins to be interspersed with pine trees as you draw nearer the forest.
6.5	*CAUTION:* cattle catcher. Officially enter Fremont National Forest.
6.85	Intersection with USFS 2916/2917: Silver Creek to your right, BPA substation to your left. **Continue straight** on USFS 28. Begin about 2 miles of incline, some of which is at a 7% grade.
9.8	Cross the National Recreation Trail. This scenic trail is accessible to non-motorized transport including hikers, horses, and mountain bikes. Hager Mountain is 4 miles to your left up this trail.
11.85	After a sign indicating sharp curves, you come to a **Y** in the road. The left fork of the **Y**, USFS 012, is an unpaved access road to Hager Mountain. **Continue straight**, on the right fork, on USFS 28. Begin an incline.
14.3	Paved road intersects on the right; this is the 1-1/2 mile access road to East Bay Campground (USFS 014). Rest room facilities available at the campground. USFS 3006 goes off to the left. **Continue straight** on USFS. 28.
14.4	*CAUTION:* cattle catcher. Road narrows to one lane, but remains well-paved.
16.3	Cross Benny Creek.
16.8	Begin a 0.3 mile 6% uphill grade.
18.0	Begin a 0.3 mile 5% downhill grade—straight, no curves, fun!
18.85	Cross Squaw Creek.
19.05	**T**-intersection; yield sign. USFS 28 goes to the left toward Paisley. **Turn right** on USFS 3142 toward Thompson Reservoir. This segment of the ride takes you through the flat sagebrush meadow of Thompson Valley.
22.05	As the road curves right to head north, you **merge into** USFS 27. USFS 27 South forks off behind you toward Bly. Continue straight ahead toward Thompson Reservoir.
23.85	Sign describing PANORAMA OF MULTIPLE-USE THOMPSON RESERVOIR AREA on the right.
24.8	Creek crossing.

25.7	Right-hand intersection, access to Thompson Reservoir Campground (1 mile). Note that this road (USFS 021) turns to gravel. **Continue straight.**
26.2	Short, steep rise.
26.8	*CAUTION:* cattle catcher.
27.3	Left intersection with road leading toward Alder Spring.
29.2	Begin a winding downhill through the West Fork Silver Creek watershed area.
30.1	Intersection with National Recreation Trail. On your right is Silver Creek Marsh Campground and trailhead. Restroom facilities.
30.7	Begin a winding uphill.
30.9	Fork in the road. Left fork goes toward Antler Trailhead and Antelope Flat. **Continue straight** on the right fork, USFS 27.
31.1	Left intersection with USFS 2804.
31.35	Right intersection with USFS 2917.
34.4	Exit Fremont National Forest. You are now on Lake County Road 4-11.
35.2	*CAUTION:* cattle catcher.
35.3	Begin the ride's best downhill—9% grade for 0.3 miles.
36.75	*CAUTION:* cattle catcher. Back out into open desert, leaving the forest behind.
39.0	*CAUTION:* cattle catcher.
39.3	Left intersection with road to USFS airstrip.
39.45	*CAUTION:* cattle catcher. As you approach the intersection with Hwy. 31, you can see the tall blue water tower on your right rising out of the Forest Service compound.
40.6	Stop-sign intersection with Hwy. 31. **Turn right.**
40.8	Cross Silver Creek.
41.0	**Turn right** toward Ranger Station.
41.1	*CAUTION:* cattle catcher.
41.3	*CAUTION:* cross the final cattle catcher. End of ride.

Other Activities In and Around the Route Area

This ride is named for the town of Silver Lake, not the lake itself, which is essentially a dry bed about 8 miles east on Highway 31. If you are looking for a lake, try Thompson Reservoir, located in Fremont National Forest in the center of our ride. When water levels allow, boats can be launched on Thompson Reservoir, and it is fished for trout and large mouth bass (levels tend to decrease late in the season due to irrigation). Birdwatchers will love the reservoir area, where loons, grebes, bald eagles, cormorants, osprey, nuthatches, woodpeckers, and many other resident and seasonal species can be viewed. Camping is available on the reservoir at East Bay Campground (17 modern, no-hook-up sites, fee charged) and Thompson Reservoir Campground (a more primitive site, no fees). Just up the road on Forest Service Road 27, Silver Creek Marsh Campground also provides campsites. For more information, contact the Silver Lake Ranger District at 541-576-2107.

The Silver Lake Ranger District also operates two rental cabins, the Fremont Point Cabin and the Hager Mountain Lookout. The latter is an actual fire lookout, and is therefore available for rent only in the fall and winter seasons. The Fremont Point Cabin is a primitive cabin with beds and cots for four people, a wood stove, and propane lighting and cooking. Users must bring their own drinking water, propane, sleeping bags, food, etc. It is not accessible by vehicle, and is a "pack-it-in, pack-it-out" facility. Contact the Ranger District for more information and reservations.

More conventional lodgings can be found in Christmas Valley or at a small motel in Silver Lake. Silver Lake also offers RV sites with hook-ups and showers (541-576-2201).

The Silver Lake area is rich in geological treasures. Be sure to visit Fort Rock State Park and Monument, some 36 miles north of Silver Lake. The rock is a circular volcanic outcropping which was the site of cave homes of some of America's earliest inhabitants. Carbon dating has shown sandals found in the caves to be at least 9000 years old. Nearby, across county road 5-10, is the Fort Rock Homestead Village Museum, a showcase of early pioneer life.

Other natural features nearby include the aptly named Hole-in-the-Ground and Crack-in-the-Ground. Hole-in-the-Ground is a mile-wide, 300-feet-deep volcanic explosion crater resembling Arizona's meteorite crater. No trees grow inside this huge crater. Crack-in-the-Ground is a 2-mile-long open fissure, 40 feet deep and about 10 feet across. A walking path winds through the crevice, affording up-close views of the unusual outcroppings on the walls.

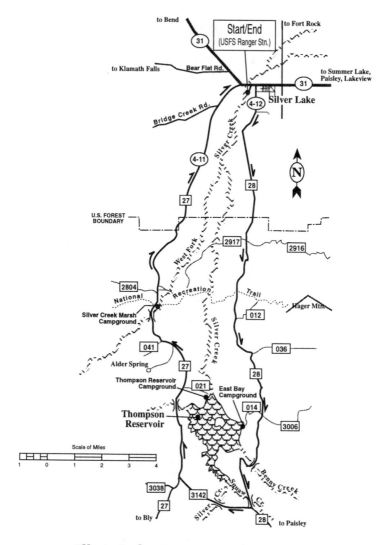

Silver Lake Forest Loop

■ Intermediate — 41.3 miles

ᗡᕼᑯ **25** ᗡᕼᑯ
Lakeview Out-and-Back

▲ Challenging — 65.0 miles
Winding, with significant hills.

Highlights

Community of Lakeview, hamlet of Adel, Warner Canyon Ski Area, Old Perpetual geyser, challenging hills, and forested canyon scenery.

Route Description

Beginning and ending in Lakeview, known as the "tallest city in Oregon" for being at the highest altitude (4800 ft.) of any incorporated city along the state highway system, this ride winds east through a canyon and over a mountain pass to the tiny outpost of Adel. The route utilizes pavement that is sometimes marginal, but offers fun and challenging cycling and beautiful scenery as it passes through Fremont National Forest and along the routes of Camas Creek, Parsnip Creek, and Deep Creek.

Thanks to Doug Troutman of the Bureau of Land Management for defining passable and impassable roads in the area, to Eleanor Giese and crew at the Fremont National Park Forest Headquarters for providing tourism information and going beyond the call of duty to research weather conditions. Special thanks to gentleman and cowboy poet Leon Flick for helping a damsel in distress during one of the worst storms of 1995.

Start

Begin at the Lakeview Ranger Station of the Fremont National Forest, just north of town on Highway 395/140. Across the street is Hunter's RV Park, with gas, camping, restaurant, and mini-mart facilities. Inquire inside the ranger station for the best place to park your vehicle.

⓪Ϥ Mileage Log

0.0	Leave the ranger station parking lot, **turning right** (north) on Hwy. 395/140.
0.1	Access road to Hunter's Hot Springs complex on your left (motel, lounge, gift shop, restaurant). Home of "Old Perpetual," the world's only continuously spouting geyser. You won't have to wait long for the show—it blows some 60 feet in the air every 90 seconds. Proceed out of town at a slight uphill grade for the first 2.5 miles.
2.0	WARNER CANYON SKI AREA sign, indicating an upcoming turn.
2.7	**Turn right** on Hwy. 140 East, toward Adel, Plush, and Winnemucca.
3.7	Lake County Road 217 intersects, and Hwy. 140 begins to wind and climb up into the forest toward the ski summit (approx. 3-1/2 miles). Pavement can be patchy and rough as you climb up into the canyon. The road is shoulderless and without guardrails, and you are sharing it with eastbound vehicle traffic likely not accustomed to cyclists; ride cautiously and defensively.
5.4	Top of the first climb.
5.65	ENTERING FREMONT NATIONAL FOREST monument sign. Road continues to ascend and wind.
7.25	WARNER CANYON SKI AREA entrance, followed by a steep 1/2-mile climb to the WARNER PASS SUMMIT, ELEVATION 5846. After the summit, descend into a meadowed valley. Exercise caution on the downhill, as the road drops off sharply, has no shoulders, and has infrequent guardrails.
10.1	Milepost marker 7; road takes a bend to the left and continues across another flat section of meadow.
10.3	S. Warner Rd. (U.S. Forest Service Rd. 3915) intersects to the right, crossing Camas Creek and leading toward Big Valley, Willow Creek Campground, and Deep Creek Campground. **Continue straight** ahead on Hwy. 140.
10.75	Cross Rosa Creek.
11.75	Intersect with Summit Prairie Rd./USFS 3910 on the right, leading toward Horse Prairie, and N. Warner Rd./USFS 3615 on the left, leading toward Honey Creek and Mud Creek Campground.
12.8	BOWERS BRIDGES CREEK sign.
13.5	Begin a 7/8 mile climb; Camas Creek valley off to your right.
14.5	LEAVING FREMONT NATIONAL FOREST sign.

16.1	Cross Mud Creek. Mud Creek joins Camas Creek, which continues to flow alongside the roadway on the right. Scenery through this section is sagebrush desert, the pavement is patchy and rough, and the roadway is winding but flat.
19.0	Cross Blue Creek.
19.5	Fork in the road. Left fork goes uphill and toward Plush and the Hart Mountain Refuge (see *Other Activities*); **continue straight** on the main road toward Adel and Winnemucca.
20.6	Begin a straight 1/2-mile climb.
21.3	Begin a winding mile-long 6% downhill grade. Good pavement. This begins an essentially downhill 11+ miles into Adel.
22.0	Cross Parsnip Creek. Road continues to wind and is flat or gently declining for next three miles.
25.1	Cross Drake Creek. Begin a 0.3 mile, fairly steep uphill.
25.8	Pull-out area on the right overlooking Deep Creek. The resulting canyon vista is dramatic.
25.9	First of two imitation cattle catchers painted on the roadway. Road winds downhill toward the level of Deep Creek, which remains visible to your right and continues to flank the road as you wind into Adel.
26.0	Second "cattle catcher." (These are painted only; no danger to cyclists.,
32.4	Arrive at Adel, which consists of a gas station/restaurant/tavern/ convenience store combo and an RV park. If you continued straight on Hwy. 140, it would lead toward Winnemucca, Nevada. Turning left would put you on Lake County Rd. 3-10, also known as Hogback Rd., which leads to the hamlet of Plush and to the Warner Valley and Warner Lakes. **Turn right** into Adel on Lake County Rd. 3-14.
32.5	**Turn around** at the convenience store. This offers the only "rest and refueling" stop on the route. Rest rooms are for customers only, but you can choose between ordering lunch, playing a quick game of pool, and just picking up a candy bar or some aspirin. Leave Adel the way you came in, turning left on Hwy. 140 and going up the 3-mile initial hill into Deep Creek canyon. Be prepared for about 11 miles of uphill before things flatten out.
35.4	Depending upon the current water level, a nice view of Deep Creek's waterfall on your left.
38.7	Pull-out on the left with a footpath leading to the creek.
39.0	First of the pair of imitation cattle catchers painted on roadway.

39.1	Second cattle catcher.
39.9	Cross Drake Creek, then up a fairly steep 0.3 mile hill, followed by a couple miles of flat before you resume climbing.
43.0	Cross Parsnip Creek, then ascend a mile-long 6% uphill grade. This is the end of the ascent out of Adel.
45.5	The Plush Cutoff Rd. intersects on the right.
46.0	Cross Blue Creek.
48.9	Cross Mud Creek just before it joins Camas Creek. The latter flows along the left side of the road as you continue west.
50.5	Just after you begin an ascent, you will see the FREMONT NATIONAL FOREST sign.
52.2	Bowers Bridges Creek.
53.25	Intersection with N. Warner Rd., etc.
54.25	Cross Rosa Creek.
54.65	S. Warner Rd. intersects to the left.
56.3	Begin a winding ascent toward the Warner Canyon Ski Area.
57.2	WARNER PASS SUMMIT, ELEVATION 5846. Almost immediately after the summit, Warner Canyon Ski Area is visible on the left as you begin to wind downhill.
57.7	Entrance to Warner Canyon Ski Area parking lot on your left. Continue a long, winding downhill for almost 5 miles until the next highway junction.
59.3	LEAVING FREMONT NATIONAL FOREST monument marker on your left.
61.3	Left-hand intersection with Lake County Rd. 217.
62.2	Stop-sign intersection with Hwy. 395. **Turn left** on Hwy. 140 West/395 South, toward Lakeview/Klamath Falls. It's a straight shot back into north Lakeview. Watch for "Old Perpetual" to spout ahead and to your right.
64.9	Entrance to Hunter Hot Springs complex on your right.
65.0	Ranger station on your left; end of ride.

Other Activities In and Around the Route Area

Situated at the junction of highways 395 and 140, Lakeview offers restaurants and lodgings for the benefit of the weary traveler. An "All-America City" finalist in 1988, Lakeview is a proud little community with friendly, helpful residents and a laid-back attitude.

The Chamber of Commerce and many other city and county offices (Lakeview is the seat of vast Lake County) are located downtown on North F Street, phone 541-947-6040. An office of the Bureau of Land Management, located at 1000 South Ninth Street (P.O. Box 151), or phone 541-947-2177, is another helpful source of information, as is the Lakeview Ranger Station (from which you begin the ride) and the Fremont National Forest Headquarters, about 1/2 mile south of the Ranger Station toward town.

Lakeview is known as the Hang Gliding Capital of the West, with outstanding thermals and perfect launch sites just outside of town. Developed sites near Lakeview include Black Cap, Tague's Butte, Daughtery Slide, Hadley Butte, and Sugar Hill. For more information, contact the Chamber.

Northeast of Adel, off Hogback Road, is Hart Mountain National Antelope Refuge, a 270,000-acre haven for prong-horned antelope and California Bighorn sheep. Information and viewing maps are available at the headquarters on the mountain's upland plateau, or write Hart Mountain National Antelope Refuge, P.O. Box 111, Lakeview, OR 97630(541-947-3315.)

Traveling north from Lakeview on Highway 395, you will skirt Lake Abert, unique in its salt biosphere. Dominated by two lowly resident species—the brine shrimp and the alkali fly—it is also a stopover for many species of migratory birds. Abert is the third largest salt sea in America, after Great Salt Lake and Salton Sea. Towering 2000 feet above you as you pass the lake is Abert Rim, a 30-mile-long fault scarp.

Highway 31 between this Lakeview ride and the Silver Lake Forest Loop (ride 24) offers many sites of historical and geological interest. Well-preserved petroglyphs can be viewed at Picture Rock Pass, giving further evidence of the existence of aboriginal Americans in this area dating back as much as 14,000 years ago. Summer Lake is a recreational lake with a hot springs at the south end and a nearby wildlife area that is home to mule deer, antelope, elk, and golden and bald eagles. Bighorn sheep can be spotted on adjacent Winter Ridge, which also affords breathtaking vistas and was a historic point in the passage of pioneer settlers.

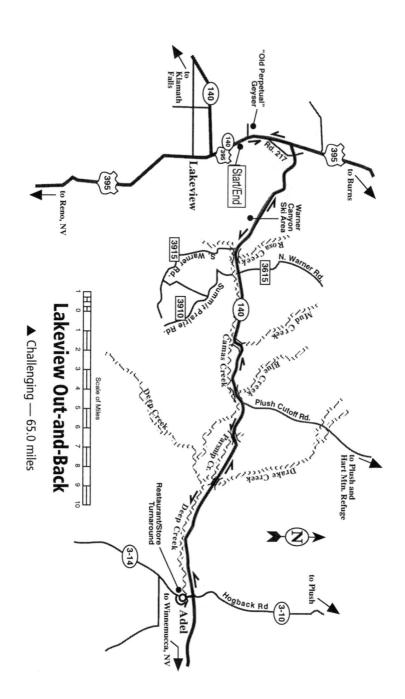

Good Phone Numbers to Know

Eastern Oregon Visitors Association	1-541-523-9200 (office)
	1-800-332-1843 (brochures)
Idaho Tourism Information	1-800-635-7820
Oregon Tourism Commission	1-800-547-7842
Washington State Department of Community, Trade & Economic Development, Tourism Division	1-360-586-2088
Washington State Lodging & Travel Guide	1-800-544-1800

Numbers for various Chambers of Commerce and other entities specific to a particular ride are listed within that ride description.

Author Notes

Sally O'Neal Coates is a writer and musician living in Richland, Washington. Her household includes her husband, Doug, stepson, Mitchell, and an assortment of livestock. She is co-founder of the mid-life rock group Final Brain Cell, and her greatest ambition is to become a best-selling author so she can rock out with Amy Tan, Stephen King, Barbara Kingsolver, and Dave Barry in the Rock Bottom Remainders.

Index